ECONOMIC COMMISSION FOR EUROPE
Geneva

ENVIRONMENTAL
CONVENTIONS

elaborated under the auspices of the
United Nations Economic Commission for Europe

UNITED NATIONS
New York and Geneva, 1994

NOTE

Symbols of United Nations documents are composed of capital letters combined with figures. Mention of such a symbol indicates a reference to a United Nations document.

UNITED NATIONS PUBLICATION

Sales No. E.93.II.E.35

ISBN 92-1-116583-0

PREFACE

While the region of the United Nations Economic Commission for Europe (ECE) is marked by considerably different levels of economic development and natural-resource endowment, it shares a number of important socio-economic characteristics and common environmental assets. The region represents more than two-thirds of world trade. A great share of modern technology is developed, manufactured, and marketed by the countries of the region. On the other hand, the region accounts for more than three-quarters of global pollution and is the heaviest consumer of natural resources and energy. This has placed a great responsibility on ECE countries for environmental protection, sustainable development and a rational use of natural resources.

Addressing these problems, mostly transboundary in nature, represents an important and urgent task, which can only be accomplished by closer and more effective cooperation among Governments of the region to ensure that activities under their control do not damage the environment of other States or areas beyond their national jurisdiction. In this context, the need for regional legally binding instruments on topical environmental issues is becoming ever more important.

The current process of dramatic change in Europe is posing new and compelling challenges to regional cooperation in general and to cooperation in the field of the environment in particular. Between 1990 and January 1994, ECE membership increased from thirty-four to fifty-four countries,* including twenty-six countries in transition from a centrally planned to a market economy. However, not only has the number of ECE members increased, the very nature of the Commission is also changing profoundly. The fact that a growing number of countries in transition are at the level of developing countries will also increase the diversity of socio-economic and environmental backgrounds of ECE members and therefore of the challenges facing the Commission in the field of environment. One of the greatest challenges today is how to develop and apply legally binding instruments, especially in view of the increasing membership, for the region as a whole.

The response of ECE countries to this challenge has been swift and productive. By various Commission deci-

sions and through Ministerial Declarations, member Governments have attached special importance to the ECE as a forum not only for the elaboration of such instruments in the field of environment, but in particular for relevant follow-up action to implement them and thus to help bridge the current gaps between the conditions under which traditional market economies and countries in transition have to cope with environmental problems. Cooperation in the field of environment has developed into one of the priority activities of the Commission. Sustainable Development is a guiding principle for its work in all sectors (transport, trade, energy, industry, agriculture and timber, and human settlements).

The United Nations Economic Commission for Europe continues to be the sole pan-European forum for environmental cooperation and sustainable development where countries from western, central and eastern Europe, North America and Israel are represented on an equal footing. The important role of the ECE has also been recognized within the framework of the process of the Conference on Security and Cooperation in Europe (CSCE), where CSCE participating States have, on several occasions, called upon the ECE to prepare legal instruments in the field of environment and to further strengthen cooperation on specific environmental topics.

During the last 15 years, eight international legally binding instruments, four conventions and four protocols, have been developed in the ECE on air pollution, environmental impact assessment, industrial accidents and transboundary waters. The importance of these legal instruments as effective tools to promote active, direct and action-oriented international cooperation at the regional level is growing in view of the Commission's increasing membership, the many new borderlines cutting through Europe and, hence, the growing potential for transboundary environmental problems. These treaties, which are important elements of a common European legal framework, are concrete and effective instruments to eliminate the former dividing line between east and west and to integrate countries with economies in transition into a pan-European legal and economic space.

However, these conventions would not fully achieve their purpose if they were to remain mere expressions of goodwill on the part of member States. The significance of the legal instruments agreed upon within the ECE lies in the fact that they are rapidly and efficiently implemented and complied with by as many member countries as possible, and translated into practical rules and regulations at the national level.

Regarding compliance monitoring of these conventions, steps are being taken by the Commission in the light of the Ministerial Declaration of the Conference ''Environment for Europe'' (Lucerne, Switzerland, April

---

* ECE member countries (18 January 1994): Albania; Andorra; Armenia; Austria; Azerbaijan; Belarus; Belgium; Bosnia and Herzegovina; Bulgaria; Canada; Croatia; Cyprus; Czech Republic; Denmark; Estonia; Finland; France; Georgia; Germany; Greece; Hungary; Iceland; Ireland; Israel; Italy; Kazakhstan; Kyrgyzstan; Latvia; Liechtenstein; Lithuania; Luxembourg; Malta; Monaco; Netherlands; Norway; Poland; Portugal; Republic of Moldova; Romania; Russian Federation; San Marino; Slovakia; Slovenia; Spain; Sweden; Switzerland; The former Yugoslav Republic of Macedonia; Turkey; Turkmenistan; Ukraine; United Kingdom of Great Britain and Northern Ireland; United States of America; Uzbekistan; Yugoslavia.

1993) to review implementation and verification measures, taking into account the negotiating history of each convention and the specific problems of the countries in transition, for presentation to the Signatories or Parties to these conventions. In the ongoing negotiations for a second sulphur protocol under the Convention on Long-range Transboundary Air Pollution, considerable attention is paid to the introduction of stringent compliance provisions.

The present publication contains the nucleus of a regional environmental legal framework for ECE countries. The Convention on Long-range Transboundary Air Pollution and three of its four protocols have already entered into force as efficient instruments for the abatement of transboundary air pollutants. A second generation of protocols is emerging; it will focus on pollution control, based on the concepts of critical loads and cost-effectiveness. Three other conventions, the Convention on Environmental Impact Assessment in a Transboundary Context, the Convention on the Transboundary Effects of Industrial Accidents and the Convention on the Protection and Use of Transboundary Watercourses and International Lakes, are in the process of ratification. The Commission has called on all ECE member States and the European Community to consider, if they had not already done so, ratification of or accession to these conventions, as appropriate. This will help to make them fully operational on a region-wide level as soon as possible and will ensure that environmental considerations do not slip down the list of national priorities. It is very encouraging that Signatories to these conventions have taken steps to implement the respective conventions to the maximum extent possible pending their entry into force which, it is hoped, will happen in the near future.

The legal instruments contained in this compendium also provide elements and approaches which could be of assistance to the countries of other regions of the world in their respective campaigns to halt and reduce environmental degradation and to promote sustainable development. They represent an important element of the contribution that the ECE region will have to make in order to meet the objectives of Agenda 21 adopted by all United Nations member countries at the "Earth Summit" in Rio de Janeiro, Brazil, in 1992.

CONTENTS

LIST OF ABBREVIATIONS

Besides the common abbreviations, symbols and terms, the following have been used in this publication:

Currencies

DM	Deutsche mark
ECU	European currency unit
US$	United States dollar

Organizations, conferences and centres

CSCE	Conference on Security and Cooperation in Europe
ECE	Economic Commission for Europe
ILO	International Labour Organisation
MSC-W	Meteorological Synthesizing Centre-West
SAPRC	Statewide Air Pollution Research Center, Los Angeles, United States of America
UNEP	United Nations Environment Programme

Programmes

APELL	Awareness and Preparedness for Emergencies at Local Level
EMEP	Cooperative Programme for Monitoring and Evaluation of the Long-range Transmission of Air Pollutants in Europe

Weights and measures

C	Celsius
g	Gram
GJ	Gigajoule
h	Hour
kg	Kilogram
km	Kilometre
km^2	Square kilometre
kPa	Kilopascal
kW_{el}	Kilowatt (electric)
kWh	Kilowatt-hour
l	Litre
m^2	Square metre
m^3	Cubic metre
mg	Milligram
MW	Megawatt
MW_{el}	Megawatt (electric)
MW_{th}	Megawatt (thermal)
t	Tonne

Technical and scientific abbreviations

AC	Activated carbon process
BBF	Biased-burner-firing
BCF	Bioconcentration factor
BE	Bitumen emulsion
BFBC	Bubbling fluidized bed combustion
BOOS	Burner-out-of-service
CCGT	Combined cycle gas turbine
CFBC	Circulating fluidized bed combustion
CFC	Chlorofluorocarbon
CNG	Compressed natural gas
CO	Carbon monoxide
CO_2	Carbon dioxide
DBB	Dry bottom boiler
EC	Effective concentration
EGR	Exhaust gas recirculation
FBC	Fluidized bed combustion
FGR	Flue gas recirculation
IC	Inhibiting concentration
IC engine	Internal combustion engine
IFNR	In-furnace-NO_x-reduction reburning
IGCC	Integrated gasification combined cycle
LC	Lethal concentration
LD	Lethal dose
LEA	Low excess air combustion
LNB	Low NO_x burner
LPG	Liquefied petroleum gas
MIR	Maximum Incremental Reactivity
NH_3	Ammonia
NO	Nitrogen oxide
NO_2	Nigrogen dioxide
NO_x	Nitrogen oxides
N_2O	Dinitrogen monoxide
O_3	Ozone
OBD	On-board diagnostic system
OFA	Over fire air combustion
PF	Pulverized fuel
PFBC	Pressurized fluidized bed combustion
POCP	Photochemical ozone creation potential
Pow	Partition coefficient octanol/water
ppb	Parts per billion
ppmv	Parts per million by volume
RAP	Reduced air preheat
RVP	Reid vapour pressure
SCR	Selective catalytic reduction
SNCR	Selective non-catalytic reduction
SO_2	Sulphur dioxide
SO_3	Sulphur trioxide
SO_x	Sulphur oxides
STP	Standard temperature (0°C) and pressure (1.013 x 10^5 Pa)
TOMA	Tropospheric ozone management area
UV	Ultraviolet
VOC	Volatile organic compound
WBB	Wet bottom boiler

CONVENTION ON LONG-RANGE TRANSBOUNDARY AIR POLLUTION

CONVENTION ON LONG-RANGE TRANSBOUNDARY AIR POLLUTION

The Parties to the present Convention,

Determined to promote relations and cooperation in the field of environmental protection,

Aware of the significance of the activities of the United Nations Economic Commission for Europe in strengthening such relations and cooperation, particularly in the field of air pollution including long-range transport of air pollutants,

Recognizing the contribution of the Economic Commission for Europe to the multilateral implementation of the pertinent provisions of the Final Act of the Conference on Security and Cooperation in Europe,

Cognizant of the references in the chapter on environment of the Final Act of the Conference on Security and Cooperation in Europe calling for cooperation to control air pollution and its effects, including long-range transport of air pollutants, and to the development through international cooperation of an extensive programme for the monitoring and evaluation of long-range transport of air pollutants, starting with sulphur dioxide and with possible extension to other pollutants,

Considering the pertinent provisions of the Declaration of the United Nations Conference on the Human Environment, and in particular principle 21, which expresses the common conviction that States have, in accordance with the Charter of the United Nations and the principles of international law, the sovereign right to exploit their own resources pursuant to their own environmental policies, and the responsibility to ensure that activities within their jurisdiction or control do not cause damage to the environment of other States or of areas beyond the limits of national jurisdiction,

Recognizing the existence of possible adverse effects, in the short and long term, of air pollution including transboundary air pollution,

Concerned that a rise in the level of emissions of air pollutants within the region as forecast may increase such adverse effects,

Recognizing the need to study the implications of the long-range transport of air pollutants and the need to seek solutions for the problems identified,

Affirming their willingness to reinforce active international cooperation to develop appropriate national policies and by means of exchange of information, consultation, research and monitoring, to coordinate national action for combating air pollution including long-range transboundary air pollution,

Have agreed as follows:

DEFINITIONS

Article 1

For the purposes of the present Convention:

(*a*) "*Air pollution*" means the introduction by man, directly or indirectly, of substances or energy into the air resulting in deleterious effects of such a nature as to endanger human health, harm living resources and ecosystems and material property and impair or interfere with amenities and other legitimate uses of the environment, and "air pollutants" shall be construed accordingly;

(*b*) "*Long-range transboundary air pollution*" means air pollution whose physical origin is situated wholly or in part within the area under the national jurisdiction of one State and which has adverse effects in the area under the jurisdiction of another State at such a distance that it is not generally possible to distinguish the contribution of individual emission sources or groups of sources.

FUNDAMENTAL PRINCIPLES

Article 2

The Contracting Parties, taking due account of the facts and problems involved, are determined to protect man and his environment against air pollution and shall endeavour to limit and, as far as possible, gradually reduce and prevent air pollution including long-range transboundary air pollution.

Article 3

The Contracting Parties, within the framework of the present Convention, shall by means of exchanges of information, consultation, research and monitoring, develop without undue delay policies and strategies which shall serve as a means of combating the discharge of air pollutants, taking into account efforts already made at national and international levels.

Article 4

The Contracting Parties shall exchange information on and review their policies, scientific activities and technical measures aimed at combating, as far as possible, the discharge of air pollutants which may have adverse effects, thereby contributing to the reduction of air pollution including long-range transboundary air pollution.

Article 5

Consultations shall be held, upon request, at an early stage between, on the one hand, Contracting Parties which are actually affected by or exposed to a significant risk of long-range transboundary air pollution and, on the other hand, Contracting Parties within which and subject to whose jurisdiction a significant contribution to long-range transboundary air pollution originates, or could originate, in connection with activities carried on or contemplated therein.

AIR QUALITY MANAGEMENT

Article 6

Taking into account articles 2 to 5, the ongoing research, exchange of information and monitoring and the results thereof, the cost and effectiveness of local and other remedies and, in order to combat air pollution, in particular that originating from new or rebuilt installations, each Contracting Party undertakes to develop the best policies and strategies including air quality management systems and, as part of them, control measures compatible with balanced development, in particular by using the best available technology which is economically feasible and low- and non-waste technology.

RESEARCH AND DEVELOPMENT

Article 7

The Contracting Parties, as appropriate to their needs, shall initiate and cooperate in the conduct of research into and/or development of:

(a) Existing and proposed technologies for reducing emissions of sulphur compounds and other major air pollutants, including technical and economic feasibility, and environmental consequences;

(b) Instrumentation and other techniques for monitoring and measuring emission rates and ambient concentrations of air pollutants;

(c) Improved models for a better understanding of the transmission of long-range transboundary air pollutants;

(d) The effects of sulphur compounds and other major air pollutants on human health and the environment, including agriculture, forestry, materials, aquatic and other natural ecosystems and visibility, with a view to establishing a scientific basis for dose/effect relationships designed to protect the environment;

(e) The economic, social and environmental assessment of alternative measures for attaining environmental objectives including the reduction of long-range transboundary air pollution;

(f) Education and training programmes related to the environmental aspects of pollution by sulphur compounds and other major air pollutants.

EXCHANGE OF INFORMATION

Article 8

The Contracting Parties, within the framework of the Executive Body referred to in article 10 and bilaterally, shall, in their common interests, exchange available information on:

(a) Data on emissions at periods of time to be agreed upon, of agreed air pollutants, starting with sulphur dioxide, coming from grid-units of agreed size; or on the fluxes of agreed air pollutants, starting with sulphur dioxide, across national borders, at distances and at periods of time to be agreed upon;

(b) Major changes in national policies and in general industrial development, and their potential impact, which would be likely to cause significant changes in long-range transboundary air pollution;

(c) Control technologies for reducing air pollution relevant to long-range transboundary air pollution;

(d) The projected cost of the emission control of sulphur compounds and other major air pollutants on a national scale;

(e) Meteorological and physico-chemical data relating to the processes during transmission;

(f) Physico-chemical and biological data relating to the effects of long-range transboundary air pollution and the extent of the damage[1] which these data indicate can be attributed to long-range transboundary air pollution;

(g) National, subregional and regional policies and strategies for the control of sulphur compounds and other major air pollutants.

IMPLEMENTATION AND FURTHER DEVELOPMENT OF THE CO-OPERATIVE PROGRAMME FOR THE MONITORING AND EVALUATION OF THE LONG-RANGE TRANSMISSION OF AIR POLLUTANTS IN EUROPE

Article 9

The Contracting Parties stress the need for the implementation of the existing "Cooperative programme for the monitoring and evaluation of the long-range transmission of air pollutants in Europe" (hereinafter referred to as EMEP) and, with regard to the further development of this programme, agree to emphasize:

(a) The desirability of Contracting Parties joining in and fully implementing EMEP which, as a first step, is based on the monitoring of sulphur dioxide and related substances;

---

[1] The present Convention does not contain a rule on State liability as to damage.

(*b*) The need to use comparable or standardized procedures for monitoring whenever possible;

(*c*) The desirability of basing the monitoring programme on the framework of both national and international programmes. The establishment of monitoring stations and the collection of data shall be carried out under the national jurisdiction of the country in which the monitoring stations are located;

(*d*) The desirability of establishing a framework for a cooperative environmental monitoring programme, based on and taking into account present and future national, subregional, regional and other international programmes;

(*e*) The need to exchange data on emissions at periods of time to be agreed upon, of agreed air pollutants, starting with sulphur dioxide, coming from grid-units of agreed size; or on the fluxes of agreed air pollutants, starting with sulphur dioxide, across national borders, at distances and at periods of time to be agreed upon. The method, including the model, used to determine the fluxes, as well as the method, including the model, used to determine the transmission of air pollutants based on the emissions per grid-unit, shall be made available and periodically reviewed, in order to improve the methods and the models;

(*f*) Their willingness to continue the exchange and periodic updating of national data on total emissions of agreed air pollutants, starting with sulphur dioxide;

(*g*) The need to provide meteorological and physico-chemical data relating to processes during transmission;

(*h*) The need to monitor chemical components in other media such as water, soil and vegetation, as well as a similar monitoring programme to record effects on health and environment;

(*i*) The desirability of extending the national EMEP networks to make them operational for control and surveillance purposes.

EXECUTIVE BODY

Article 10

1. The representatives of the Contracting Parties shall, within the framework of the Senior Advisers to ECE Governments on Environmental Problems, constitute the Executive Body of the present Convention, and shall meet at least annually in that capacity.

2. The Executive Body shall:

(*a*) Review the implementation of the present Convention;

(*b*) Establish, as appropriate, working groups to consider matters related to the implementation and development of the present Convention and to this end to prepare appropriate studies and other documentation and to submit recommendations to be considered by the Executive Body;

(*c*) Fulfil such other functions as may be appropriate under the provisions of the present Convention.

3. The Executive Body shall utilize the Steering Body for the EMEP to play an integral part in the operation of the present Convention, in particular with regard to data collection and scientific cooperation.

4. The Executive Body, in discharging its functions, shall, when it deems appropriate, also make use of information from other relevant international organizations.

SECRETARIAT

Article 11

The Executive Secretary of the Economic Commission for Europe shall carry out, for the Executive Body, the following secretariat functions:

(*a*) To convene and prepare the meetings of the Executive Body;

(*b*) To transmit to the Contracting Parties reports and other information received in accordance with the provisions of the present Convention;

(*c*) To discharge the functions assigned by the Executive Body.

AMENDMENTS TO THE CONVENTION

Article 12

1. Any Contracting Party may propose amendments to the present Convention.

2. The text of proposed amendments shall be submitted in writing to the Executive Secretary of the Economic Commission for Europe, who shall communicate them to all Contracting Parties. The Executive Body shall discuss proposed amendments at its next annual meeting provided that such proposals have been circulated by the Executive Secretary of the Economic Commission for Europe to the Contracting Parties at least ninety days in advance.

3. An amendment to the present Convention shall be adopted by consensus of the representatives of the Contracting Parties, and shall enter into force for the Contracting Parties which have accepted it on the ninetieth day after the date on which two-thirds of the Contracting Parties have deposited their instruments of acceptance with the depositary. Thereafter, the amendment shall enter into force for any other Contracting Party on the ninetieth day after the date on which that Contracting Party deposits its instrument of acceptance of the amendment.

SETTLEMENT OF DISPUTES

Article 13

If a dispute arises between two or more Contracting Parties to the present Convention as to the interpretation or application of the Convention, they shall seek a solution by negotiation or by any other method of dispute settlement acceptable to the parties to the dispute.

SIGNATURE

Article 14

1. The present Convention shall be open for signature at the United Nations Office at Geneva from 13 to 16 November 1979 on the occasion of the High-level Meeting within the framework of the Economic Commission for Europe on the Protection of the Environment, by the member States of the Economic Commission for Europe as well as States having consultative status with the Economic Commission for Europe, pursuant to paragraph 8 of Economic and Social Council resolution 36 (IV) of 28 March 1947, and by regional economic integration organizations, constituted by sovereign States members of the Economic Commission for Europe, which have competence in respect of the negotiation, conclusion and application of international agreements in matters covered by the present Convention.

2. In matters within their competence, such regional economic integration organizations shall, on their own behalf, exercise the rights and fulfil the responsibilities which the present Convention attributes to their member States. In such cases, the member States of these organizations shall not be entitled to exercise such rights individually.

RATIFICATION, ACCEPTANCE, APPROVAL AND ACCESSION

Article 15

1. The present Convention shall be subject to ratification, acceptance or approval.

2. The present Convention shall be open for accession as from 17 November 1979 by the States and organizations referred to in article 14, paragraph 1.

3. The instruments of ratification, acceptance, approval or accession shall be deposited with the Secretary-General of the United Nations, who will perform the functions of the depositary.

ENTRY INTO FORCE

Article 16

1. The present Convention shall enter into force on the ninetieth day after the date of deposit of the twenty-fourth instrument of ratification, acceptance, approval or accession.

2. For each Contracting Party which ratifies, accepts or approves the present Convention or accedes thereto after the deposit of the twenty-fourth instrument of ratification, acceptance, approval or accession, the Convention shall enter into force on the ninetieth day after the date of deposit by such Contracting Party of its instrument of ratification, acceptance, approval or accession.

WITHDRAWAL

Article 17

At any time after five years from the date on which the present Convention has come into force with respect to a Contracting Party, that Contracting Party may withdraw from the Convention by giving written notification to the depositary. Any such withdrawal shall take effect on the ninetieth day after the date of its receipt by the depositary.

AUTHENTIC TEXTS

Article 18

The original of the present Convention, of which the English, French and Russian texts are equally authentic, shall be deposited with the Secretary-General of the United Nations.

IN WITNESS WHEREOF the undersigned, being duly authorized thereto, have signed the present Convention.

DONE at Geneva, this thirteenth day of November one thousand nine hundred and seventy-nine.

PROTOCOL TO THE 1979 CONVENTION ON LONG-RANGE TRANSBOUNDARY AIR POLLUTION ON LONG-TERM FINANCING OF THE COOPERATIVE PROGRAMME FOR MONITORING AND EVALUATION OF THE LONG-RANGE TRANSMISSION OF AIR POLLUTANTS IN EUROPE (EMEP)

PROTOCOL TO THE 1979 CONVENTION ON LONG-RANGE TRANSBOUNDARY AIR POLLUTION ON LONG-TERM FINANCING OF THE COOPERATIVE PROGRAMME FOR MONITORING AND EVALUATION OF THE LONG-RANGE TRANSMISSION OF AIR POLLUTANTS IN EUROPE (EMEP)

The Contracting Parties,

Recalling that the Convention on Long-range Transboundary Air Pollution (hereinafter referred to as "the Convention") entered into force on 16 March 1983,

Aware of the importance of the "Cooperative programme for the monitoring and evaluation of the long-range transmission of air pollutants in Europe" (hereinafter referred to as EMEP), as provided for in Articles 9 and 10 of the Convention,

Cognizant of the positive results achieved so far in the implementation of EMEP,

Recognizing that the implementation of EMEP has hitherto been made possible by financial means provided by the United Nations Environment Programme (UNEP) and by voluntary contributions from Governments,

Bearing in mind that since the UNEP contribution will continue only until the end of 1984, and that since this contribution together with the voluntary contributions from Governments have been inadequate to support fully the EMEP work plan, it will therefore be necessary to provide for long-term funding after 1984,

Considering the appeal of the Economic Commission for Europe to ECE member Governments, contained in its decision B (XXXVIII), to make available, on a basis to be agreed at the first meeting of the Executive Body for the Convention (hereinafter referred to as the "Executive Body"), the financial resources to enable the Executive Body to carry out its activities, in particular as regards the work of EMEP,

Noting that the Convention does not contain any provisions for financing EMEP and that it is, therefore, necessary to make appropriate arrangements regarding this matter,

Considering the elements to guide the drafting of a formal instrument supplementing the Convention, as listed in recommendations adopted by the Executive Body at its first session (7-10 June 1983),

Have agreed as follows:

Article 1

DEFINITIONS

For the purposes of the present Protocol:

1. "UN assessment rate" means a Contracting Party's rate for the financial year in question in the scale of assessments for the apportionment of the expenses of the United Nations.

2. "Financial year" means the financial year of the United Nations, and "annual basis" and "annual costs" shall be construed accordingly.

3. "General Trust Fund" means the General Trust Fund for the Financing of the Implementation of the Convention on Long-range Transboundary Air Pollution, which has been established by the Secretary-General of the United Nations.

4. "Geographical scope of EMEP" means the area within which, coordinated by the international centres of EMEP,[a] monitoring is carried out.

Article 2

FINANCING OF EMEP

The financing of EMEP shall cover the annual costs of the international centres cooperating within EMEP for the activities appearing in the work programme of the Steering Body of EMEP.

Article 3

CONTRIBUTIONS

1. In accordance with the provisions of this article the financing of EMEP shall consist of mandatory contributions, supplemented by voluntary contributions. Contributions may be made in convertible currency, non-convertible currency, or in kind.

---

[a] The international centres are at present: the Chemical Coordinating Centre, the Meteorological Synthesizing Centre—East and the Meteorological Synthesizing Centre—West.

2.   Mandatory contributions shall be made on an annual basis by all Contracting Parties to the present Protocol which are within the geographical scope of EMEP.

3.   Voluntary contributions may be made by the Contracting Parties or Signatories to the present Protocol, even if their territory lies outside the geographical scope of EMEP, as well as, subject to approval by the Executive Body, on the recommendation of the Steering Body of EMEP, by any other country, organization or individual which wishes to contribute to the work programme.

4.   The annual costs of the work programme shall be covered by the mandatory contributions. Contributions in cash and in kind, such as those provided by host countries for international centres, shall be specified in the work programme. Voluntary contributions may, subject to the approval by the Executive Body, on the recommendation of the Steering Body, be utilized either for reducing the mandatory contributions or for financing specific activities within the scope of EMEP.

5.   Mandatory and voluntary contributions in cash shall be deposited in the General Trust Fund.

Article 4

SHARING OF COSTS

1.   Mandatory contributions shall be made in accordance with the terms of the Annex to the present Protocol.

2.   The Executive Body shall consider the need to amend the Annex:

(a) If the annual budget of EMEP increases by a factor of two and a half times the level of the annual budget adopted for the year of entry into force of the present Protocol or for the year of last amendment of the Annex, whichever is later; or

(b) If the Executive Body, on the recommendation of the Steering Body, designates a new international centre; or

(c) Six years after the entry into force of the present Protocol, or six years after last amendment to the Annex, whichever is later.

3.   Amendments to the Annex shall be adopted by consensus of the Executive Body.

Article 5

ANNUAL BUDGET

An annual budget for EMEP shall be drawn up by the Steering Body of EMEP, and shall be adopted by the Executive Body not later than one year in advance of the financial year to which it applies.

Article 6

AMENDMENTS TO THE PROTOCOL

1.   Any Contracting Party to the present Protocol may propose amendments to it.

2.   The text of proposed amendments shall be submitted in writing to the Executive Secretary of the Economic Commission for Europe, who shall communicate them to all Contracting Parties to the Protocol. The Executive Body shall discuss the proposed amendments at its next annual meeting provided that such proposals have been circulated by the Executive Secretary of the Economic Commission for Europe to the Contracting Parties to the Protocol at least ninety days in advance.

3.   An amendment to the present Protocol, other than an amendment to its Annex, shall be adopted by consensus of the representatives of the Contracting Parties to the Protocol and shall enter into force for the Contracting Parties to the Protocol which have accepted it on the ninetieth day after the day on which two-thirds of those Contracting Parties have deposited with the depositary their instruments of acceptance of the amendment. The amendment shall enter into force for any other Contracting Party on the ninetieth day after the date on which that Contracting Party deposits its instrument of acceptance of the amendment.

Article 7

SETTLEMENT OF DISPUTES

If a dispute arises between two or more Contracting Parties to the present Protocol as to its interpretation or application, they shall seek a solution by negotiation or by any other method of dispute settlement acceptable to the parties to the dispute.

Article 8

SIGNATURE

1.   The present Protocol shall be open for signature at the United Nations Office in Geneva from 28 September 1984 until 5 October 1984 inclusive, then at the Headquarters of the United Nations in New York until 4 April 1985, by the member States of the Economic Commission for Europe as well as States having consultative status with the Economic Commission for Europe, pursuant to paragraph 8 of Economic and Social Council resolution 36 (IV) of 28 March 1947, and by regional economic integration organizations, constituted by sovereign States members of the Economic Commission for Europe, which have competence in respect of the negotiation, conclusion and application of international agreements in matters covered by the present Protocol, provided that the States and organizations concerned are parties to the Convention.

2.   In matters within their competence, such regional economic integration organizations shall, on their own behalf, exercise the rights and fulfil the responsibilities which the present Protocol attributes to their member States. In such cases, the member States of these organizations shall not be entitled to exercise such rights individually.

Article 9

RATIFICATION, ACCEPTANCE, APPROVAL AND ACCESSION

1.   The present Protocol shall be subject to ratification, acceptance or approval by Signatories.

2.   The present Protocol shall be open for accession as from 5 October 1984 by the States and Organizations referred to in article 8, paragraph 1.

3.   The instruments of ratification, acceptance, approval or accession shall be deposited with the Secretary-General of the United Nations, who will perform the functions of the depositary.

Article 10

ENTRY INTO FORCE

1.   The present Protocol shall enter into force on the ninetieth day following the date on which:

(*a*) Instruments of ratification, acceptance, approval or accession have been deposited by at least nineteen States and Organizations referred to in article 8, paragraph 1, which are within the geographical scope of EMEP; and

(*b*) The aggregate of the UN assessment rates for such States and Organizations exceeds 40 per cent.

2.   For each State and Organization referred to in article 8, paragraph 1, which ratifies, accepts or approves the present Protocol or accedes thereto after the requirements for entry into force laid down in paragraph 1 above have been met, the Protocol shall enter into force on the ninetieth day after the date of deposit by such State or Organization of its instrument of ratification, acceptance, approval or accession.

Article 11

WITHDRAWAL

1.   At any time after five years from the date on which the present Protocol has come into force with respect to a Contracting Party, that Contracting Party may withdraw from it by giving written notification to the depositary. Any such withdrawal shall take effect on the ninetieth day after the date of its receipt by the depositary.

2.   Withdrawal shall not affect the financial obligations of the withdrawing Party until the date on which the withdrawal takes effect.

Article 12

AUTHENTIC TEXTS

The original of the present Protocol, of which the English, French and Russian texts are equally authentic, shall be deposited with the Secretary-General of the United Nations.

IN WITNESS WHEREOF the undersigned, being duly authorized thereto, have signed the present Protocol.

DONE at Geneva, this twenty-eighth day of September one thousand nine hundred and eighty-four.

Annex referred to in article 4 of the Protocol to the 1979 Convention on Long-range Transboundary Air Pollution on Long-term Financing of the Cooperative Programme for Monitoring and Evaluation of the Long-range Transmission of Air Pollutants in Europe (EMEP)

Mandatory contributions for sharing of costs for financing the Cooperative Programme for Monitoring and Evaluation of the Long-range Transmission of Air Pollutants in Europe (EMEP) shall, from 1994, be calculated according to the following scale*

	Per cent
Austria	1.59
Belarus	0.71
Bulgaria	0.35
Croatia	0.15
Cyprus	0.04
Czech Republic*	
Finland	1.07
Holy See	0.02
Hungary	0.45
Iceland	0.06
Liechtenstein	0.02
Norway	1.13
Poland	1.42
Romania	0.37
Russian Federation	20.78
San Marino	0.02
Slovak Republic[a]	
Slovenia	0.10
Sweden	2.66
Switzerland	2.26
Turkey	0.60
Ukraine	2.60
Yugoslavia	0.23

Member countries of the European Community:

Belgium	2.36
Denmark	1.38
France	11.99
Germany	18.47
Greece	1.00
Ireland	0.50
Italy	6.89
Luxembourg	0.10
Netherlands	3.28
Portugal	0.30
Spain	3.54
United Kingdom	8.61
European Community	3.33
TOTAL	98.38

* The order in which the Contracting Parties are listed in this Annex is specifically made in relation to the cost-sharing system agreed upon by the Executive Body for the Convention. Accordingly, the listing is a feature which is specific to the Protocol on the financing of EMEP.

[a] The former Czechoslovakia had an agreed share of 1.54 per cent.

PROTOCOL TO THE 1979 CONVENTION ON LONG-RANGE TRANSBOUNDARY AIR POLLUTION ON THE REDUCTION OF SULPHUR EMISSIONS OR THEIR TRANSBOUNDARY FLUXES BY AT LEAST 30 PER CENT

PROTOCOL TO THE 1979 CONVENTION ON LONG-RANGE TRANSBOUNDARY AIR POLLUTION ON THE REDUCTION OF SULPHUR EMISSIONS OR THEIR TRANSBOUNDARY FLUXES BY AT LEAST 30 PER CENT

The Parties,

Determined to implement the Convention on Long-range Transboundary Air Pollution,

Concerned that the present emissions of air pollutants are causing widespread damage, in exposed parts of Europe and North America, to natural resources of vital environmental and economic importance, such as forests, soils and waters, and to materials (including historical monuments) and, under certain circumstances, have harmful effects on human health,

Aware of the fact that the predominant sources of air pollution contributing to the acidification of the environment are the combustion of fossil fuels for energy production, and the main technological processes in various industrial sectors, as well as transport, which lead to emissions of sulphur dioxide, nitrogen oxides, and other pollutants,

Considering that high priority should be given to reducing sulphur emissions, which will have positive results environmentally, on the overall economic situation and on human health,

Recalling the decision of the United Nations Economic Commission for Europe (ECE) at its thirty-ninth session, which stresses the urgency of intensifying efforts to arrive at coordinated national strategies and policies in the ECE region to reduce sulphur emissions effectively at national levels,

Recalling the recognition by the Executive Body for the Convention at its first session of the need to decrease effectively the total annual emissions of sulphur compounds or their transboundary fluxes by 1993-1995, using 1980 levels as the basis for calculations of reductions,

Recalling that the Multilateral Conference on the Causes and Prevention of Damage to Forests and Water by Air Pollution in Europe (Munich, 24-27 June 1984) had requested that the Executive Body for the Convention, as a matter of highest priority, adopt a proposal for a specific agreement on the reduction of annual national sulphur emissions or their transboundary fluxes by 1993 at the latest,

Noting that a number of Contracting Parties to the Convention have decided to implement reductions of their national annual sulphur emissions or their transboundary fluxes by at least 30 per cent as soon as possible and at the latest by 1993, using 1980 levels as the basis for calculation of reductions,

Recognizing, on the other hand, that some Contracting Parties to the Convention, while not signing the present Protocol at the time of its opening for signature, will nevertheless contribute significantly to the reduction of transboundary air pollution, or will continue to make efforts to control sulphur emissions, as stated in the document annexed to the report of the Executive Body at its third session,

Have agreed as follows:

Article 1

DEFINITIONS

For the purposes of the present Protocol,

1. "Convention" means the Convention on Long-range Transboundary Air Pollution, adopted in Geneva on 13 November 1979;

2. "EMEP" means the Cooperative Programme for Monitoring and Evaluation of the Long-range Transmission of Air Pollutants in Europe;

3. "Executive Body" means the Executive Body for the Convention constituted under article 10, paragraph 1 of the Convention;

4. "Geographical scope of EMEP" means the area defined in article 1, paragraph 4 of the Protocol to the 1979 Convention on Long-range Transboundary Air Pollution on Long-term Financing of the Cooperative Programme for Monitoring and Evaluation of the Long-range Transmission of Air Pollutants in Europe (EMEP), adopted in Geneva on 28 September 1984;

5. "Parties" means, unless the context otherwise requires, the Parties to the present Protocol.

Article 2

BASIC PROVISIONS

The Parties shall reduce their national annual sulphur emissions or their transboundary fluxes by at least 30 per cent as soon as possible and at the latest by 1993, using 1980 levels as the basis for calculation of reductions.

Article 3

FURTHER REDUCTIONS

The Parties recognize the need for each of them to study at the national level the necessity for further reductions, beyond those referred to in article 2, of sulphur emissions or their transboundary fluxes when environmental conditions warrant.

Article 4

REPORTING OF ANNUAL EMISSIONS

Each Party shall provide annually to the Executive Body its levels of national annual sulphur emissions, and the basis upon which they have been calculated.

Article 5

CALCULATIONS OF TRANSBOUNDARY FLUXES

EMEP shall in good time before the annual meetings of the Executive Body provide to the Executive Body calculations of sulphur budgets and also of transboundary fluxes and depositions of sulphur compounds for each previous year within the geographical scope of EMEP, utilizing appropriate models. In areas outside the geographical scope of EMEP, models appropriate to the particular circumstances of Parties therein shall be used.

Article 6

NATIONAL PROGRAMMES, POLICIES AND STRATEGIES

The Parties shall, within the framework of the Convention, develop without undue delay national programmes, policies and strategies which shall serve as a means of reducing sulphur emissions or their transboundary fluxes, by at least 30 per cent as soon as possible and at the latest by 1993, and shall report thereon as well as on progress towards achieving the goal to the Executive Body.

Article 7

AMENDMENTS TO THE PROTOCOL

1. Any Party may propose amendments to the present Protocol.

2. Proposed amendments shall be submitted in writing to the Executive Secretary of the Economic Commission for Europe who shall communicate them to all Parties. The Executive Body shall discuss the proposed amendments at its next annual meeting provided that such proposals have been circulated by the Executive Secretary of the Economic Commission for Europe to the Parties at least 90 days in advance.

3. An amendment to the present Protocol shall be adopted by consensus of the representatives of the Parties, and shall enter into force for the Parties which have accepted it on the ninetieth day after the date on which two-thirds of the Parties have deposited their instruments of acceptance of the amendment. The amendment shall enter into force for any other Party on the ninetieth day after the date on which that Party deposits its instrument of acceptance of the amendment.

Article 8

SETTLEMENT OF DISPUTES

If a dispute arises between two or more Parties as to the interpretation or application of the present Protocol, they shall seek a solution by negotiation or by any other method of dispute settlement acceptable to the parties to the dispute.

Article 9

SIGNATURE

1. The present Protocol shall be open for signature at Helsinki (Finland) from 8 July 1985 until 12 July 1985 inclusive, by the member States of the Economic Commission for Europe as well as States having consultative status with the Economic Commission for Europe, pursuant to paragraph 8 of Economic and Social Council resolution 36 (IV) of 28 March 1947, and by regional economic integration organizations, constituted by sovereign States members of the Economic Commission for Europe, which have competence in respect of the negotiation, conclusion and application of international agreements in matters covered by the present Protocol, provided that the States and organizations concerned are Parties to the Convention.

2. In matters within their competence, such regional economic integration organizations shall, on their own behalf, exercise the rights and fulfil the responsibilities which the present Protocol attributes to their member States. In such cases, the member States of these organizations shall not be entitled to exercise such rights individually.

Article 10

RATIFICATION, ACCEPTANCE, APPROVAL AND ACCESSION

1. The present Protocol shall be subject to ratification, acceptance or approval by Signatories.

2. The present Protocol shall be open for accession as from 13 July 1985 by the States and organizations referred to in article 9, paragraph 1.

3. A State or organization acceding to the present Protocol after its entry into force shall implement article 2 at the latest by 1993. However, if the Protocol is acceded to after 1990, article 2 may be implemented later than 1993 by the Party concerned but not later than 1995, and such a Party shall implement article 6 correspondingly.

4. The instruments of ratification, acceptance, approval or accession shall be deposited with the Secretary-General of the United Nations, who will perform the functions of depositary.

Article 11

ENTRY INTO FORCE

1. The present Protocol shall enter into force on the ninetieth day following the date on which the sixteenth instrument of ratification, acceptance, approval or accession has been deposited.

2. For each State and organization referred to in article 9, paragraph 1, which ratifies, accepts or approves the present Protocol or accedes thereto after the deposit of the sixteenth instrument of ratification, acceptance, approval, or accession, the Protocol shall enter into force on the ninetieth day after the date of deposit by such Party of its instrument of ratification, acceptance, approval, or accession.

Article 12

WITHDRAWAL

At any time after five years from the date on which the present Protocol has come into force with respect to a Party, that Party may withdraw from it by giving written notification to the depositary. Any such withdrawal shall take effect on the ninetieth day after the date of its receipt by the depositary.

Article 13

AUTHENTIC TEXTS

The original of the present Protocol, of which the English, French and Russian texts are equally authentic, shall be deposited with the Secretary-General of the United Nations.

IN WITNESS WHEREOF the undersigned, being duly authorized thereto, have signed the present Protocol.

DONE at Helsinki this eighth day of July one thousand nine hundred and eighty-five.

PROTOCOL TO THE 1979 CONVENTION ON LONG-RANGE TRANSBOUNDARY AIR POLLUTION CONCERNING THE CONTROL OF EMISSIONS OF NITROGEN OXIDES OR THEIR TRANSBOUNDARY FLUXES

PROTOCOL TO THE 1979 CONVENTION ON LONG-RANGE TRANSBOUNDARY AIR POLLUTION CONCERNING THE CONTROL OF EMISSIONS OF NITROGEN OXIDES OR THEIR TRANSBOUNDARY FLUXES

The Parties,

Determined to implement the Convention on Long-range Transboundary Air Pollution,

Concerned that present emissions of air pollutants are causing damage, in exposed parts of Europe and North America, to natural resources of vital environmental and economic importance,

Recalling that the Executive Body for the Convention recognized at its second session the need to reduce effectively the total annual emissions of nitrogen oxides from stationary and mobile sources or their transboundary fluxes by 1995, and the need on the part of other States that had already made progress in reducing these emissions to maintain and review their emission standards for nitrogen oxides,

Taking into consideration existing scientific and technical data on emissions, atmospheric movements and effects on the environment of nitrogen oxides and their secondary products, as well as on control technologies,

Conscious that the adverse environmental effects of emissions of nitrogen oxides vary among countries,

Determined to take effective action to control and reduce national annual emissions of nitrogen oxides or their transboundary fluxes by, in particular, the application of appropriate national emission standards to new mobile and major new stationary sources and the retro-fitting of existing major stationary sources,

Recognizing that scientific and technical knowledge of these matters is developing and that it will be necessary to take such developments into account when reviewing the operation of this Protocol and deciding on further action,

Noting that the elaboration of an approach based on critical loads is aimed at the establishment of an effect-oriented scientific basis to be taken into account when reviewing the operation of this Protocol and at deciding on further internationally agreed measures to limit and reduce emissions of nitrogen oxides or their transboundary fluxes,

Recognizing that the expeditious consideration of procedures to create more favourable conditions for exchange of technology will contribute to the effective reduction of emissions of nitrogen oxides in the region of the Commission,

Noting with appreciation the mutual commitment undertaken by several countries to implement immediate and substantial reductions of national annual emissions of nitrogen oxides,

Acknowledging the measures already taken by some countries which have had the effect of reducing emissions of nitrogen oxides,

Have agreed as follows:

Article 1

DEFINITIONS

For the purposes of the present Protocol,

1. "Convention" means the Convention on Long-range Transboundary Air Pollution, adopted in Geneva on 13 November 1979;

2. "EMEP" means the Cooperative Programme for Monitoring and Evaluation of the Long-range Transmission of Air Pollutants in Europe;

3. "Executive Body" means the Executive Body for the Convention constituted under article 10, paragraph 1 of the Convention;

4. "Geographical scope of EMEP" means the area defined in article 1, paragraph 4 of the Protocol to the 1979 Convention on Long-range Transboundary Air Pollution on Long-term Financing of the Cooperative Programme for Monitoring and Evaluation of the Long-range Transmission of Air Pollutants in Europe (EMEP), adopted in Geneva on 28 September 1984;

5. "Parties" means, unless the context otherwise requires, the Parties to the present Protocol;

6. "Commission" means the United Nations Economic Commission for Europe;

7. "Critical load" means a quantitative estimate of the exposure to one or more pollutants below which significant harmful effects on specified sensitive elements of the environment do not occur according to present knowledge;

8. "Major existing stationary source" means any existing stationary source the thermal input of which is at least 100 MW;

9. "Major new stationary source" means any new stationary source the thermal input of which is at least 50 MW;

10. "Major source category" means any category of sources which emit or may emit air pollutants in the form of nitrogen oxides, including the categories described in the Technical Annex, and which contribute at least 10 per cent of the total national emissions of nitrogen oxides on an annual basis as measured or calculated in the first calendar year after the date of entry into force of the present Protocol, and every fourth year thereafter;

11. "New stationary source" means any stationary source the construction or substantial modification of which is commenced after the expiration of two years from the date of entry into force of this Protocol;

12. "New mobile source" means a motor vehicle or other mobile source which is manufactured after the expiration of two years from the date of entry into force of the present Protocol.

Article 2

BASIC OBLIGATIONS

1. The Parties shall, as soon as possible and as a first step, take effective measures to control and/or reduce their national annual emissions of nitrogen oxides or their transboundary fluxes so that these, at the latest by 31 December 1994, do not exceed their national annual emissions of nitrogen oxides or transboundary fluxes of such emissions for the calendar year 1987 or any previous year to be specified upon signature of, or accession to, the Protocol, provided that in addition, with respect to any Party specifying such a previous year, its national average annual transboundary fluxes or national average annual emissions of nitrogen oxides for the period from 1 January 1987 to 1 January 1996 do not exceed its transboundary fluxes or national emissions for the calendar year 1987.

2. Furthermore, the Parties shall in particular, and no later than two years after the date of entry into force of the present Protocol:

(a) Apply national emissions standards to major new stationary sources and/or source categories, and to substantially modified stationary sources in major source categories, based on the best available technologies which are economically feasible, taking into consideration the Technical Annex;

(b) Apply national emission standards to new mobile sources in all major source categories based on the best available technologies which are economically feasible, taking into consideration the Technical Annex and the relevant decisions taken within the framework of the Inland Transport Committee of the Commission; and

(c) Introduce pollution control measures for major existing stationary sources, taking into consideration the Technical Annex and the characteristics of the plant, its age and its rate of utilization and the need to avoid undue operational disruption.

3. (a) The Parties shall, as a second step, commence negotiations, no later than six months after the date of entry into force of the present Protocol, on further steps to reduce national annual emissions of nitrogen oxides or transboundary fluxes of such emissions, taking into account the best available scientific and technological developments, internationally accepted critical loads and other elements resulting from the work programme undertaken under article 6.

(b) To this end, the Parties shall cooperate in order to establish:

(i) Critical loads;

(ii) Reductions in national annual emissions of nitrogen oxides or transboundary fluxes of such emissions as required to achieve agreed objectives based on critical loads; and

(iii) Measures and a timetable commencing no later than 1 January 1996 for achieving such reductions.

4. Parties may take more stringent measures than those required by the present article.

Article 3

EXCHANGE OF TECHNOLOGY

1. The Parties shall, consistent with their national laws, regulations and practices, facilitate the exchange of technology to reduce emissions of nitrogen oxides, particularly through the promotion of:

(a) Commercial exchange of available technology;

(b) Direct industrial contacts and cooperation, including joint ventures;

(c) Exchange of information and experience; and

(d) Provision of technical assistance.

2. In promoting the activities specified in subparagraphs (a) to (d) above, the Parties shall create favourable conditions by facilitating contacts and cooperation among appropriate organizations and individuals in the private and public sectors that are capable of providing technology, design and engineering services, equipment or finance.

3. The Parties shall, no later than six months after the date of entry into force of the present Protocol, commence consideration of procedures to create more favourable conditions for the exchange of technology to reduce emissions of nitrogen oxides.

Article 4

UNLEADED FUEL

The Parties shall, as soon as possible and no later than two years after the date of entry into force of the present Protocol, make unleaded fuel sufficiently available, in particular cases as a minimum along main international transit routes, to facilitate the circulation of vehicles equipped with catalytic converters.

Article 5

REVIEW PROCESS

1. The Parties shall regularly review the present Protocol, taking into account the best available scientific substantiation and technological development.

2. The first review shall take place no later than one year after the date of entry into force of the present Protocol.

Article 6

WORK TO BE UNDERTAKEN

The Parties shall give high priority to research and monitoring related to the development and application of an approach based on critical loads to determine, on a scientific basis, necessary reductions in emissions of nitrogen oxides. The Parties shall, in particular, through national research programmes, in the work plan of the Executive Body and through other cooperative programmes within the framework of the Convention, seek to:

(a) Identify and quantify effects of emissions of nitrogen oxides on humans, plant and animal life, waters, soils and materials, taking into account the impact on these of nitrogen oxides from sources other than atmospheric deposition;

(b) Determine the geographical distribution of sensitive areas;

(c) Develop measurements and model calculations including harmonized methodologies for the calculation of emissions, to quantify the long-range transport of nitrogen oxides and related pollutants;

(d) Improve estimates of the performance and costs of technologies for control of emissions of nitrogen oxides and record the development of improved and new technologies; and

(e) Develop, in the context of an approach based on critical loads, methods to integrate scientific, technical and economic data in order to determine appropriate control strategies.

Article 7

NATIONAL PROGRAMMES, POLICIES AND STRATEGIES

The Parties shall develop without undue delay national programmes, policies and strategies to implement the obligations under the present Protocol that shall serve as a means of controlling and reducing emissions of nitrogen oxides or their transboundary fluxes.

Article 8

INFORMATION EXCHANGE AND ANNUAL REPORTING

1. The Parties shall exchange information by notifying the Executive Body of the national programmes, policies and strategies that they develop in accordance with article 7 and by reporting to it annually on progress achieved under, and any changes to, those programmes, policies and strategies, and in particular on:

(a) The levels of national annual emissions of nitrogen oxides and the basis upon which they have been calculated;

(b) Progress in applying national emission standards required under article 2, subparagraphs 2 (a) and 2 (b), and the national emission standards applied or to be applied, and the sources and/or source categories concerned;

(c) Progress in introducing the pollution control measures required under article 2, subparagraph 2 (c), the sources concerned and the measures introduced or to be introduced;

(d) Progress in making unleaded fuel available;

(e) Measures taken to facilitate the exchange of technology; and

(f) Progress in establishing critical loads.

2. Such information shall, as far as possible, be submitted in accordance with a uniform reporting framework.

Article 9

CALCULATIONS

EMEP shall, utilizing appropriate models and in good time before the annual meetings of the Executive Body, provide to the Executive Body calculations of nitrogen budgets and also of transboundary fluxes and deposition of nitrogen oxides within the geographical scope of EMEP. In areas outside the geographical scope of EMEP, models appropriate to the particular circumstances of Parties to the Convention therein shall be used.

Article 10

TECHNICAL ANNEX

The Technical Annex to the present Protocol is recommendatory in character. It shall form an integral part of the Protocol.

Article 11

AMENDMENTS TO THE PROTOCOL

1. Any Party may propose amendments to the present Protocol.

2.   Proposed amendments shall be submitted in writing to the Executive Secretary of the Commission who shall communicate them to all Parties. The Executive Body shall discuss the proposed amendments at its next annual meeting provided that these proposals have been circulated by the Executive Secretary to the Parties at least ninety days in advance.

3.   Amendments to the Protocol, other than amendments to its Technical Annex, shall be adopted by consensus of the Parties present at a meeting of the Executive Body, and shall enter into force for the Parties which have accepted them on the ninetieth day after the date on which two-thirds of the Parties have deposited their instruments of acceptance thereof. Amendments shall enter into force for any Party which has accepted them after two-thirds of the Parties have deposited their instruments of acceptance of the amendment, on the ninetieth day after the date on which that Party deposited its instrument of acceptance of the amendments.

4.   Amendments to the Technical Annex shall be adopted by consensus of the Parties present at a meeting of the Executive Body and shall become effective thirty days after the date on which they have been communicated in accordance with paragraph 5 below.

5.   Amendments under paragraphs 3 and 4 above shall, as soon as possible after their adoption, be communicated by the Executive Secretary to all Parties.

Article 12

SETTLEMENT OF DISPUTES

If a dispute arises between two or more Parties as to the interpretation or application of the present Protocol, they shall seek a solution by negotiation or by any other method of dispute settlement acceptable to the parties to the dispute.

Article 13

SIGNATURE

1.   The present Protocol shall be open for signature at Sofia from 1 November 1988 until 4 November 1988 inclusive, then at the Headquarters of the United Nations in New York until 5 May 1989, by the member States of the Commission as well as States having consultative status with the Commission, pursuant to paragraph 8 of Economic and Social Council resolution 36 (IV) of 28 March 1947, and by regional economic integration organizations, constituted by sovereign States members of the Commission, which have competence in respect of the negotiation, conclusion and application of international agreements in matters covered by the Protocol, provided that the States and organizations concerned are Parties to the Convention.

2.   In matters within their competence, such regional economic integration organizations shall, on their own behalf, exercise the rights and fulfil the responsibilities which the present Protocol attributes to their member States. In such cases, the member States of these organizations shall not be entitled to exercise such rights individually.

Article 14

RATIFICATION, ACCEPTANCE, APPROVAL AND ACCESSION

1.   The present Protocol shall be subject to ratification, acceptance or approval by Signatories.

2.   The present Protocol shall be open for accession as from 6 May 1989 by the States and organizations referred to in article 13, paragraph 1.

3.   A State or organization which accedes to the present Protocol after 31 December 1993 may implement articles 2 and 4 no later than 31 December 1995.

4.   The instruments of ratification, acceptance, approval or accession shall be deposited with the Secretary-General of the United Nations, who will perform the functions of depositary.

Article 15

ENTRY INTO FORCE

1.   The present Protocol shall enter into force on the ninetieth day following the date on which the sixteenth instrument of ratification, acceptance, approval or accession has been deposited.

2.   For each State and organization referred to in article 13, paragraph 1, which ratifies, accepts or approves the present Protocol or accedes thereto after the deposit of the sixteenth instrument of ratification, acceptance, approval, or accession, the Protocol shall enter into force on the ninetieth day following the date of deposit by such Party of its instrument of ratification, acceptance, approval, or accession.

Article 16

WITHDRAWAL

At any time after five years from the date on which the present Protocol has come into force with respect to a Party, that Party may withdraw from it by giving written notification to the depositary. Any such withdrawal shall take effect on the ninetieth day following the date of its receipt by the depositary, or on such later date as may be specified in the notification of the withdrawal.

Article 17

AUTHENTIC TEXTS

The original of the present Protocol, of which the English, French and Russian texts are equally authentic,

shall be deposited with the Secretary-General of the United Nations.

IN WITNESS WHEREOF the undersigned, being duly authorized thereto, have signed the present Protocol.

DONE at Sofia this thirty-first day of October one thousand nine hundred and eighty-eight.

TECHNICAL ANNEX

1. The purpose of this annex is to provide guidance to the Parties to the Convention in identifying NO_x control options and techniques in the implementation of their obligations under the Protocol.

2. It is based on information on options and techniques for NO_x emission reduction and their performance and costs contained in official documentation of the Executive Body for the Convention and of the ECE Inland Transport Committee and of their subsidiary bodies.

3. The annex addresses the control of NO_x emissions considered as the sum of nitrogen oxide (NO) and nitrogen dioxide (NO_2) expressed as NO_2 and lists a number of NO_x reduction measures and techniques spanning a wide range of costs and efficiencies. Unless otherwise indicated these techniques are considered to be well established on the basis of substantial operating experience, which in most cases has been gained over five years or more. It cannot, however, be considered as an exhaustive statement of control options; its aim is to provide guidance to Parties in identifying best available technologies which are economically feasible as a basis for national emission standards and in the introduction of pollution control measures.

4. The choice of pollution control measures for any particular case will depend on a number of factors, including the relevant legislative and regulatory provisions, primary energy pattern, industrial infrastructure and economic circumstances of the Party concerned and, in the case of stationary sources, the specific circumstances of the plant. It should be borne in mind also that sources of NO_x are often sources of other pollutants as well, such as sulphur oxides (SO_x), volatile organic compounds (VOCs), and particulates. In the design of control options for such sources, all polluting emissions should be considered together in order to maximize the overall abatement effect and minimize the impact of the source on the environment.

5. The annex reflects the state of knowledge and experience of NO_x control measures, including retrofitting, which has been achieved by 1992, in the case of stationary sources, and by 1991 in the case of mobile sources. As this knowledge and this experience continuously expand, the annex needs to be updated and amended regularly.

I. CONTROL TECHNOLOGIES FOR NO_x EMISSIONS FROM STATIONARY SOURCES

6. Fossil fuel combustion is the main source of anthropogenic NO_x emissions from stationary sources. In addition, some non-combustion processes may contribute considerably to the emissions. The major stationary source categories of NO_x emissions, based on EMEP/CORINAIR'90, include:

(a) Public power, cogeneration and district heating plants:

  (i) Boilers;

  (ii) Stationary combustion turbines and internal combustion engines;

(b) Commercial, institutional and residential combustion plants:

  (i) Commercial boilers;

  (ii) Domestic heaters;

(c) Industrial combustion plants and processes with combustion:

  (i) Boilers and process heaters (no direct contact between flue gas and products);

  (ii) Processes (direct contact); (e.g. calcination processes in rotary kilns, production of cement, lime, etc., glass production, metallurgical operation, pulp production);

(d) Non-combustion processes, e.g. nitric acid production;

(e) Extraction, processing and distribution of fossil fuels;

(f) Waste treatment and disposal, e.g. incineration of municipal and industrial waste.

7. For the ECE region, combustion processes (categories (a), (b), (c)) account for 85 per cent of NO_x emissions from stationary sources. Non-combustion processes, e.g. production processes, account for 12 per cent, and extraction, processing and distribution of fossil fuels for 3 per cent of total NO_x emissions. Although in many ECE countries, power plants in category (a) are the largest stationary contributor to NO_x emissions, road traffic is usually the largest single overall source of NO_x emissions, but the distribution does vary between Parties to the Convention. Furthermore, industrial sources should be kept in mind.

GENERAL OPTIONS FOR REDUCING NO_x EMISSIONS FROM COMBUSTION

8. General options for NO_x reduction are:

(a) Energy management measures:[1]

---

[1] Options 1 (a) and (b) are integrated in the energy structure/policy of a Party. Implementation status, efficiency and costs per sector are not considered here.

   (i) Energy saving;

   (ii) Energy mix;

(b) Technical options:

   (i) Fuel switching/cleaning;

   (ii) Other combustion technologies;

   (iii) Process and combustion modifications;

   (iv) Flue gas treatment.

9. To achieve the most efficient NO_x reduction programme, beyond the measures listed in (a), a combination of technical options identified in (b) should be considered. Furthermore, the combination of combustion modification and flue gas treatment needs site specific evaluation.

10. In some cases, options for reducing NO_x emissions may also result in the reduction of emissions of CO_2 and SO_2 and other pollutants.

Energy saving

11. The rational use of energy (improved energy efficiency/process operation, cogeneration and/or demand-side management) usually results in a reduction in NO_x emissions.

Energy mix

12. In general, NO_x emissions can be reduced by increasing the proportion of non-combustion energy sources (i.e. hydro, nuclear, wind, etc.) to the energy mix. However, further environmental impacts have to be considered.

Fuel switching/cleaning

13. Table I.1 shows the uncontrolled NO_x emission levels to be expected during fossil fuel combustion for the different sectors.

14. Fuel switching (e.g. from high- to low-nitrogen fuels or from coal to gas) can lead to lower NO_x emissions but there may be certain restrictions, such as the availability of low NO_x emitting fuels (e.g. natural gas on plant level) and adaptability of existing furnaces to different fuels. In many ECE countries, some coal or oil combustion plants are being replaced by gas-fired combustion plants.

15. Fuel cleaning for fuel nitrogen removal is not a commercial option. Increasing the application of cracking technology in refineries, however, also brings about a reduction in the nitrogen content of the end-product.

Other combustion technologies

16. These are combustion technologies with improved thermal efficiency and reduced NO_x emissions. They include:

(a) Cogeneration using gas turbines and engines;

(b) Fluidized bed combustion (FBC): bubbling (BFBC) and circulating (CFBC);

(c) Integrated gasification combined cycle (IGCC);

(d) Combined cycle gas turbines (CCGT).

17. The emission levels for these techniques are summarized in table I.1.

18. Stationary combustion turbines can also be integrated into existing conventional power plants (known as topping). The overall efficiency can increase by 5 per cent to 6 per cent, but achievable NO_x reduction will depend on site and fuel specific conditions. Gas turbines and gas engines are widely applied in cogeneration applications. Typically some 30 per cent energy saving can be attained. Both have made significant progress in reducing NO_x emissions through new concepts in combustion and system technology. However, major alterations to the existing boiler system become necessary.

19. FBC is a combustion technology for burning hard coal and brown coal but it can also burn other solid fuels such as petroleum coke and low grade fuels such as waste, peat and wood. In addition, emissions can be reduced by integrated combustion control in the system. A newer concept of FBC is pressurized fluidized bed combustion (PFBC) presently being commercialized for the generation of electricity and heat. The total installed capacity of FBC has approached approximately 30,000 MW_{th} (250 to 350 plants), including 8,000 MW_{th} in the capacity range of > 50 MW_{th}.

20. The IGCC process incorporates coal gasification and combined cycle power generation, in a gas and steam turbine. The gasified coal is burned in the combustion chamber of the gas turbine. The technology also exists for heavy oil residue and bitumen emulsion. The installed capacity is presently about 1,000 MW_{el} (5 plants).

21. Combined cycle gas power stations using advanced gas turbines with an energy efficiency of 48 per cent to 52 per cent and with reduced NO_x emissions are currently being planned.

Process and combustion modifications

22. These are measures applied during combustion to reduce the formation of NO_x. They include the control of combustion air ratio, flame temperature, fuel to air ratio, etc. The following combustion techniques, either singly or in combination, are available for new and existing installations. They are widely implemented in the power plant sector and in some areas of the industrial sector:

(a) Low excess air combustion (LEA);[2]

(b) Reduced air preheat (RAP);[2]

(c) Burner-out-of-service (BOOS);[2]

(d) Biased-burner-firing (BBF);[2]

(e) Low NO_x burners (LNB);[2,3]

(f) Flue gas recirculation (FGR);[3]

(g) Over fire air combustion (OFA);[2,3]

(h) In-furnace-NO_x-reduction reburning (IFNR);[4]

---

[2] Typical retrofit measures, with limited efficiency and applicability.

[3] State-of-the-art in new plants.

[4] Implemented in single large commercial plants; operational experience still limited.

(*i*) Water/steam injection and lean/premixed combination.[5]

23. The emission levels due to the application of these techniques are summarized in table I.1 (based mainly on experience in power plants).

24. Combustion modifications have been under continuous development and optimization. In-furnace-NO_x-reduction is being tested in some large-scale demonstration plants, whereas basic combustion modifications are incorporated mainly into boiler and burner design. For example, modern furnace designs incorporate OFA ports, and gas/oil burners are equipped for flue gas recirculation. The latest generation of LNBs combines both air-staging and fuel-staging. A remarkable increase in full-scale retrofit of combustion modifications in ECE member countries has been recorded in the last years. By 1992 a total of about 150,000 MW was installed.

Flue gas treatment processes

25. Flue gas treatment processes aim at removing already formed NO_x and are also referred to as secondary measures. Wherever possible it is usual to apply primary measures as a first stage of NO_x reduction before applying flue gas treatment processes. The state-of-the-art flue gas treatment processes are all based on the removal of NO_x by dry chemical processes.

26. They are the following:

(*a*) Selective Catalytic Reduction (SCR);

(*b*) Selective Non-catalytic Reduction (SNCR);

(*c*) Combined NO_x/SO_x removal processes:

   (i) Activated Carbon Process (AC);

   (ii) Combined catalytic NO_x/SO_x removal.

27. The emission levels for SCR and SNCR are summarized in table I.1. Data are based on the practical experience gathered from a large number of implemented plants. By 1991 in the European part of the ECE about 130 SCR plants corresponding to 50,000 MW_{el}, 12 SNCR installations (2,000 MW_{el}), 1 AC plant (250 MW_{el}) and 2 combined catalytic processes (400 MW_{el}) were erected. The NO_x removal efficiency of AC and combined catalytic processes are similar to SCR.

28. Table I.1 also summarizes the costs of applying the NO_x abatement technologies.

CONTROL TECHNIQUES FOR OTHER SECTORS

29. Unlike most combustion processes, the application of combustion and/or process modifications in the industrial sector has many process specific limitations. In cement kilns or glass melting furnaces, for example, certain high temperatures are necessary to ensure the product quality. Typical combustion modifications being used are staged combustion/low NO_x burners, flue gas recirculation and process optimization (e.g. precalcination in cement kilns).

---

[5] For combustion turbines.

30. Some examples are given in table I.1.

SIDE-EFFECTS/BY-PRODUCTS

31. The following side-effects will not prevent the implementation of any technology or method, but should be considered when several NO_x abatement options are possible. However, in general, these side-effects can be limited by proper design and operation:

(*a*) Combustion modifications:

   —Possible decrease in overall efficiency;

   —Increased CO formation and hydrocarbon emissions;

   —Corrosion due to reducing atmosphere;

   —Possible N_2O formation in FBC systems;

   —Possible increase of carbon fly ash;

(*b*) SCR:

   —NH_3 in the fly ash;

   —Formation of ammonium salts on downstream facilities;

   —Deactivation of catalyst;

   —Increased conversion of SO_2 to SO_3;

(*c*) SNCR:

   —NH_3 in the fly ash;

   —Formation of ammonium salts on downstream facilities;

   —Possible formation of N_2O.

32. In terms of by-products, deactivated catalysts from the SCR process are the only relevant products. Due to the classification as waste, a simple disposal is not possible, however recycling options exist.

33. The reagent production of ammonia and urea for flue gas treatment processes involves a number of separate steps which require energy and reactants. The storage systems for ammonia are subject to the relevant safety legislation and such systems are designed to operate as totally closed systems, with a resultant minimum of ammonia emissions. The use of NH_3 is, however, not jeopardized even when taking into account the indirect emissions related to the production and transportation of NH_3.

MONITORING AND REPORTING

34. The measures taken to carry out national strategies and policies for the abatement of air pollution include legislation and regulatory provisions, economic incentives and disincentives, as well as technological requirements (best available technology).

35. In general emission limiting standards may be set per emission source according to plant size, operating mode, combustion technology, fuel type and whether it is a new or existing plant. An alternative approach also used is to set a target for the reduction of total NO_x emis-

sions from a group of existing sources and to allow the Parties to choose where to take action to reach this target (bubble concept).

36. The limiting of the NO_x emissions to the levels set out in the national framework legislation has to be controlled by a permanent monitoring and reporting system and reported to the supervising authorities.

37. Several monitoring systems, using both continuous and discontinuous measurement methods, are available. However quality requirements vary among Parties. Measurements are to be carried out by qualified institutes and approved measuring/monitoring systems. To this end a certification system would provide the best assurance.

38. In the framework of modern automated monitoring systems and process control equipment, reporting creates no problems. The collection of data for further use is a state-of-the-art technique. However, data to be reported to competent authorities differ from Party to Party. To obtain better comparability, data sets and prescribing regulations should be harmonized. Harmonization is also desirable for quality assurance of measuring/monitoring systems. This should be taken into account when comparing data from different Parties.

39. To avoid discrepancies and inconsistencies, key issues and parameters including the following, must be well-defined:

Definition of the standards expressed as ppmv, mg/m^3, g/GJ, kg/h or kg/t of products. Most of these units need to be calculated and need specification in terms of gas temperature, humidity, pressure, oxygen content or heat input value;

Definition of time over which standards may be averaged, expressed as hours, months or a year;

Definition of failure times and corresponding emergency regulations regarding bypass of monitoring systems or shut-down of the installation;

Definition of methods for backfilling of data missed or lost as a result of equipment failure;

Definition of the parameter set to be measured. Depending on the type of industrial process, the necessary information may differ. This also involves the location of the measurement point within the system.

40. Quality control of measurements must be ensured.

TABLE I.1

| Energy source | Uncontrolled Emissions | | Process and Combustion Modifications | | | Flue Gas Treatment | | | | | |
| | | | | | | (a) Non-catalytic | | | (b) Catalytic (after primary measures) | | |
	mg/m^{3} [1]	g/GJ [1]	mg/m^{3} [1]	g/GJ [1]	ECU/kW_{el} [2]	mg/m^{3} [1]	g/GJ [1]	ECU/kW_{el} [2]	mg/m^{3} [1]	g/GJ [1]	ECU/kW_{el} [2]
Source category (i): Public power, cogeneration and district heating											
Boilers:											
Coal, WBB [4]	1 500-2 200	530-770	1 000-1 800	350-630	3-25	no data		no data	< 200	< 70	50-100(125-200) [12]
Coal, DBB [5]	800-1 500	280-530	300-850	100-300	3-25	200-400	70-140	9-11	< 200	< 70	50-100(125-200) [12]
Brown coal [5]	450-750	189-315	190-300	80-126	30-40	< 200	< 84		< 200	< 85	80-100
Heavy oil [6]	700-1 400	140-400	150-500	40-140	up to 20	175-250	50-70	6-8	< 150	< 40	50-70
Light oil [6]	350-1 200	100-332	100-350	30-100	up to 20	no data		6-8	< 150	< 40	50-70
BE [14]	800		no data		no data	no data					no data
Natural gas [6]	150-600	40-170	50-200	15-60	3-20	no data		5-7	< 100	< 30	
FBC	200-700		180-400		1 400-1 600 [7]	< 130			no data		
PFBC	150-200	50-70			1 100 [7]	60			< 140	< 50	
IGCC [13]	< 600		< 100						no data		
Gas turbines + CCGT: [13,18]					Investment Cost:						
natural gas	165-310	140-270	30-150	26-130	Dry: 50-100 ECU/kW$_{el}$	NA			20	17	
diesel oil	235-430	230-370	50-200	45-175	Wet: 10-50 ECU/kW$_{el}$	NA			120-180	70	
IC Engines [4] (natural gas < 1 MW$_{el}$)	4 800-6 300	1 500-2 000	320-640	100-200							
Source category (ii): Commercial, institutional and residential combustion plants											
Coal	110-500	40-175									
Brown coal	70-400	30-160									
Light oil	180-440	50-120	130-250	35-70							
Gas	140-290	40-80	60-150	16-40	2-10						
Wood [15]	85-200	50-120	70-140	40-80							
Source category (iii): Industrial combustion plants and processes with combustion											
Industrial combustion plants:											
Coal, PF [8]	600-2 200	200-770	up to 700	up to 245							
Coal, grates [3]	150-600	50-200	up to 500	up to 175							
Brown coal	200-800	80-340									
Heavy oil [6]	400-1 000	110-280	up to 650	up to 180							
Light oil [6]	150-400	40-110	up to 250	up to 70							
Natural gas [6]	100-300	30-80	up to 150	up to 42	2-10						

Energy source	Uncontrolled Emissions		Process Modifications			Flue Gas Treatment					
						(a) Non-catalytic			(b) Catalytic (after primary measures)		
	mg/m^3[31]	kg/t[9]	mg/m^3[31]	kg/t[9]	ECU/t[2]	mg/m^3[31]	kg/t	ECU/kW_{el}[2]	mg/m^3[31]	kg/t[9]	ECU/kW_{el}[2]
Gas turbines + CCGT:[13, 18]											
natural gas	165-310		140-270	30-150	26-130 — Invest. Cost: Dry: 50-100 ECU/kW_{el} Wet: 10-50 ECU/kW_{el}	NA			20		17
diesel oil	235-430		200-370	50-200	45-175	NA			120-180		70
FBC[8]	100-700		100-600		100-200						
IC Engines (natural gas < 1 MW_{el})[4]	4 800-6 300		1 500-2 000		320-640						
Industrial processes:											
Calcination	1 000-2 000		500-800								
Glass:											
Plate glass		6 kg/t	500-2 000						<500		
Containers		2.5 kg/t									
Fibreglass		0.5 kg/t									
Industrial		4.2 kg/t									
Metals:											
Sintering	300-500[16]	1.5 kg/t							<500		
Coke ovens	1 000	1 kg/t									
Baked carbon fuels	<3 000										
Electric arc furnaces	50-200										
Paper and pulp:											
Black liquor	170[17]	(50-80 g/GJ)		(20-40 g/GJ)		60				13-20	

Source category (iv): Non-combustion processes

Energy source	Uncontrolled Emissions		Process Modifications			Flue Gas Treatment					
						(a) Non-catalytic			(b) Catalytic (after primary measures)		
	mg/m^3[31]	kg/t[9]	mg/m^3[31]	kg/t[9]	ECU/t[2]	mg/m^3[31]	kg/t	ECU/kW_{el}[2]	mg/m^3[31]	kg/t[9]	ECU/kW_{el}[2]
Nitric acid:											
Low pressure (1-2.2 bar)	5 000	16.5								0.01-0.8	
Medium pressure (2.3-8 bar)	approx. 1 000	3.3									
High pressure (8-15 bar)	<380	<1.25									
HOKO (-50 bar)	<380	<1.25									
Pickling:											
Brass		25[10]									
Stainless steel		0.3									
Carbon steel		0.1									

Source category (v): Extraction, processing and distribution of fossil fuels

Energy source	Uncontrolled Emissions		Process and Combustion Modifications			Flue Gas Treatment					
						(a) Non-catalytic			(b) Catalytic (after primary measures)		
	mg/m^3[31]	g/GJ[1]	mg/m^3[31]	g/GJ[1]	ECU/kW_{el}[2]	mg/m^3[31]	g/GJ[1]	ECU/kW_{el}[2]	mg/m^3[31]	g/GJ[1]	ECU/kW_{el}[2]
Refineries[5]	~1 000		100-700								

TABLE I.1 (continued)

Energy source	Uncontrolled Emissions		Process and Combustion Modifications			Flue Gas Treatment					
						(a) Non-catalytic			(b) Catalytic (after primary measures)		
	mg/m³[1]	g/GJ[1]	mg/m³[1]	g/GJ[19]	ECU/kW[12]	mg/m³[1]	g/GJ[1]	ECU/kW_el[2]	mg/m³[1]	g/GJ[9]	ECU/kW_el[2]
Source category (vi): Waste treatment and disposal											
Incineration[11]	250-500		200-400			<100					

1 Emissions in mg/m³ NO₂ (STP dry) resp. g/GJ thermal input. Conversion factors (mg/m³ to g/GJ) for NO₂ emissions from coal (hard coal): 0.35, coal (lignite): 0.42, oil/gas: 0.277, peat: 0.5, wood + bark: 0.588 [1 g/GJ = 3.6 mg/kWh].

2 Total investments 1 ECU = 2 DM.

3 Reduction generally achieved in combination with primary measures. Reduction efficiency between 80 and 95%.

4 At 5% O₂.

5 At 6% O₂.

6 At 3% O₂.

7 Incl. costs for boiler.

8 At 7% O₂.

9 Emissions from industrial processes are generally expressed as kg/t of product.

10 g/m² surface area.

11 At 11% O₂.

12 Tail gas SCR configuration as opposed to high dust.

13 At 15% O₂.

14 Bitumen emulsion.

15 Untreated wood only.

16 Heat recovery and gas recirculation.

17 For dry substance < 75%.

18 With supplementary firing: approximate additional thermal NO_x : 0-20 g/GJ.

NA: not applicable.

no data: technology applied, but no data available.

II. CONTROL TECHNOLOGIES FOR NO$_x$ EMISSIONS FROM MOTOR VEHICLES

Introduction

1. This annex is based on information on emission-control performance and costs contained in the official documentation of the Executive Body and its subsidiary bodies; in the report on Mobile Source NO$_x$ Emissions: Sources and Control Options, prepared for the Working Party on Air Pollution Problems; in the documentation of the ECE Inland Transport Committee and its subsidiary bodies and on supplementary information provided by governmentally designated experts.

2. The regular elaboration and amendment of this annex will be necessary in the light of continuously expanding experience with new vehicles incorporating low-emission technology and the development of alternative fuels, as well as with retrofitting, where appropriate, and other strategies for existing vehicles. The annex cannot be an exhaustive statement of technical options; its aim is to provide guidance to Parties in identifying economically feasible technologies for fulfilling their obligations under the Protocol.

Major NO$_x$ emitters from mobile sources

3. Primary mobile sources of anthropogenic NO$_x$ emissions include:

On-road vehicles:

(a) Petrol-fuelled and diesel-fuelled passenger cars;

(b) Light-duty vehicles;

(c) Heavy-duty vehicles;

(d) Motor cycles;

(e) Mopeds.

Off-road vehicles:

Agricultural, industrial and construction machinery.

Other mobile sources:

(a) Rail transport;

(b) Ships and other marine craft;

(c) Aircraft.

4. Road transport is a major source of anthropogenic NO$_x$ emissions in many countries of the Economic Commission for Europe (ECE), contributing up to two-thirds of total national emissions. Typically, current uncontrolled petrol-fuelled vehicles contribute up to two-thirds of total road transport NO$_x$ emissions in countries with no previous emission control.

5. Many countries have enacted regulations that limit the emission of pollutants from road vehicles. For off-road vehicles, rail, ships and other marine craft, agricultural, industrial and construction machinery, no NO$_x$ emission standards have been enacted by any ECE country. NO$_x$ emissions from these other sources may be substantial.

Until other data become available this annex concentrates on on-road vehicles only.

General aspects of control technology for NO$_x$ emissions from on-road vehicles

6. The road vehicles considered in this annex are passenger cars, light-duty vehicles, motor cycles, mopeds and heavy-duty vehicles.

7. This annex deals with both new and in-use vehicles, with attention primarily focused on NO$_x$ emission control for new vehicle types.

8. Cost figures for the various technologies given are manufacturing cost estimates rather than retail prices.

9. It is important to ensure that new-vehicle emission standards are maintained in service. This can be done through inspection and maintenance programmes, ensuring conformity of production, full useful-life durability, warranty of emission-control components, and recall of defective vehicles.

10. Fiscal incentives can encourage the accelerated introduction of desirable technology. Retrofit is of limited benefit for NO$_x$ reduction, and may be difficult to apply to more than a small percentage of the vehicle fleet.

11. Technologies that incorporate catalytic converters require the use of unleaded fuel, which should be made generally available.

12. The management of urban and long-distance traffic, though not elaborated in this annex, is important as an efficient additional approach to reducing NO$_x$ emissions. Measures to reduce NO$_x$ emissions and other air pollutants may include enforcement of speed limits and efficient traffic management. Key measures for traffic management aim at changing the modal split through tactical, structural, financial and restrictive elements. They will also be beneficial for the other harmful effects of traffic expansion such as noise, congestion, etc.

13. Measures to reduce NO$_x$ emissions, especially for diesel-fuelled engines, should take into account possible reverse effects on the emission of carbon monoxide, carbon dioxide and particles, and the need to meet limits for these substances.

Control technologies for NO$_x$ emissions from road vehicles

(a) Petrol- and diesel-fuelled passenger cars and light-duty vehicles

14. The main technologies for controlling NO$_x$ emissions are listed in table II.1.

15. The basis for comparison in table II.1 is technology option B, representing non-catalytic technology designed in response to the requirements of the United States for 1973/74 or of ECE regulation 15-04* pursuant

---

* Replaced by Regulation No. 83.

to the 1958 Agreement concerning the Adoption of Uniform Conditions of Approval and Reciprocal Recognition of Approval for Motor Vehicle Equipment and Parts. The table also presents typical emission levels for open- and closed-loop catalytic control as well as their cost.

16. The "uncontrolled" level (A) in table II.1 refers to the 1970 situation in the ECE region, but may still prevail in certain areas.

17. The emission level in table II.1 reflects emissions measured using standard test procedures. Emissions from vehicles on the road may differ because of the effect of, *inter alia*, ambient temperature, operating conditions (especially at higher speed), fuel properties and maintenance. However, the reduction potential indicated in table II.1 is considered representative of reductions achievable in use.

18. The most efficient currently available technology for NO_x reduction is option E. This technology achieves large reductions of NO_x, volatile organic compounds (VOC), and CO emissions.

19. In response to regulatory programmes for further NO_x emission reductions (e.g. low-emission vehicles in California), advanced closed-loop three-way catalyst systems are being developed (option F). These improvements will focus on engine management, very precise control of air-fuel ratio, heavier catalyst loading, on-board diagnostic systems (OBD) and other advanced control measures. Additional reductions may be achieved through the use of alternative fuels (e.g. CNG, LPG or oxygenated fuels—methanol or ethanol), as well as reformulated gasoline (petrol). The amount of additional reductions achieved through the use of these fuels will depend somewhat on operating conditions, maintenance and the other factors mentioned in paragraph 17 above, just as in the case of current fuels.

(*b*) Motor cycles and mopeds

20. Although actual NO_x emissions of motor cycles and mopeds are very low (e.g. with two-stroke engines), their NO_x emissions should be considered. While VOC emissions of these vehicles are going to be limited by many Parties to the Convention, their NO_x emissions may increase (e.g. with four-stroke engines). Generally the same technology options as described for petrol-fuelled passenger cars are applicable. In Austria and Switzerland, strict NO_x emission standards are already implemented.

(*c*) Heavy-duty diesel-fuelled vehicles

21. In table II.2 four technology options are summarized. The baseline engine configuration is the naturally aspirated engine. The trend is towards turbocharged engines. This trend has implications for improved baseline fuel consumption performance. Comparative estimates of consumption are therefore not included. The corresponding changes of particulate emissions have to be considered.

TABLE II.1

Emission control technologies for petrol- and diesel-fuelled passenger cars and light-duty vehicles

Technology option	NO_x emission level (%)	Estimated additional production cost* (US$)
Petrol-fuelled		
A. Uncontrolled situation	70	—
B. Engine modifications (engine design, carburation and ignition systems, air injection)	100	**
C. Open-loop catalyst	50	150-200
D. Closed-loop three-way catalyst	25	250-450***
E. Advanced closed-loop three-way catalyst	10	350-600***
F. Californian low-emission vehicles (advanced option E)	6	> 700***
Diesel-fuelled		
G. Conventional indirect injection diesel engine		40
H. Indirect injection engine with secondary injection, high injection pressures electronically controlled	30	1 000-1 200****
I. Direct injection engine with turbocharging	50	1 000-1 200****

  * Per vehicle, relative to technology option B.

  ** Costs for engine modifications from options A to B are estimated at US$ 40-100.

  *** Under technology options D, E and F, CO and VOC emissions are also substantially reduced, in addition to NO_x reductions. Technology options B and C result also in CO and VOC control.

  **** Fuel consumption is substantially reduced as compared to option G, while particulate emissions of technology option G are considerably higher.

TABLE II.2

Heavy-duty diesel engine technologies, emission performance and costs

Technology option		NO_x emission level (%)	Estimated additional production cost* (US$)
A.	Current conventional direct injection engine	100	0
B.	Turbocharged diesel engine	115	400-600
C.	Turbocharged diesel engine with intercooling	70	1 500-3 000
D.	Turbocharged diesel engine with intercooling, high-pressure fuel injection, electronically controlled fuel pump, combustion chamber and port optimalization EGR	50-60	1 500-3 000
E.	Conversion to spark ignition engine, e.g. alternative fuels such as CNG, LPG or oxygenated fuels, in combination with three-way catalytic converter	10-30	1 000-4 000

* Per vehicle, and depending on engine size relative to technology option A.

Control techniques for in-use vehicles

(a) Full useful life, recall and warranties

22. To promote durable emission-control systems, consideration should be given to emission standards that may not be exceeded for the "full useful life" of the vehicle. Surveillance programmes are needed to enforce this requirement. Under such programmes, manufacturers may be made responsible for recalling vehicles that fail to meet the required standards. They may also be required to provide warranties for emission-control components.

23. New vehicles shall not be equipped with devices which reduce the efficiency or switch off the emission-control systems during any operating conditions except conditions which are indispensable for trouble-free running (e.g. cold start).

(b) Inspection and maintenance

24. The inspection and maintenance programme has an important secondary function. It may encourage regular maintenance and discourage vehicle owners from tampering with or disabling the emission controls, both through direct enforcement and public information. Inspection should ensure that vehicles are not equipped with devices that reduce the efficiency or disable emission-control systems during operation. It should also ensure that emission-control systems have not been removed to achieve performance benefits at the expense of emissions.

25. Improved monitoring of emission control performance can be achieved by on-board diagnostic systems which monitor the functioning of emission-control components, store fault codes for further interrogation and warn the driver in the event of malfunction. For such vehicles, tailpipe emissions testing may not be sufficient and more sophisticated tests (e.g. dynamometer) may be necessary to assure proper functioning.

26. Inspection and maintenance programmes can be beneficial for all types of control technology by ensuring that new-vehicle emission levels are maintained. However, for uncontrolled vehicles, maintenance of new-vehicle specifications may lead to higher NO_x levels in service to the benefit of CO, VOC, and for diesels, particulate emissions. Conversely, for catalyst-controlled vehicles it is essential to ensure that the new-vehicle specifications and settings are maintained to avoid deterioration of all major pollutants, including NO_x.

PROTOCOL TO THE 1979 CONVENTION ON LONG-RANGE TRANSBOUNDARY AIR POLLUTION CONCERNING THE CONTROL OF EMISSIONS OF VOLATILE ORGANIC COMPOUNDS OR THEIR TRANSBOUNDARY FLUXES

PROTOCOL TO THE 1979 CONVENTION ON LONG-RANGE TRANSBOUNDARY AIR POLLUTION CONCERNING THE CONTROL OF EMISSIONS OF VOLATILE ORGANIC COMPOUNDS OR THEIR TRANSBOUNDARY FLUXES

The Parties,

Determined to implement the Convention on Long-range Transboundary Air Pollution,

Concerned that present emissions of volatile organic compounds (VOCs) and the resulting secondary photochemical oxidant products are causing damage, in exposed parts of Europe and North America, to natural resources of vital environmental and economic importance and, under certain exposure conditions, have harmful effects on human health,

Noting that under the Protocol concerning the Control of Emissions of Nitrogen Oxides or their Transboundary Fluxes, adopted in Sofia on 31 October 1988, there is already agreement to reduce emissions of oxides of nitrogen,

Recognizing the contribution of VOCs and nitrogen oxides to the formation of tropospheric ozone,

Recognizing also that VOCs, nitrogen oxides and resulting ozone are transported across international boundaries, affecting air quality in neighbouring States,

Aware that the mechanism of photochemical oxidant creation is such that the reduction of emissions of VOCs is necessary in order to reduce the incidence of photochemical oxidants,

Further aware that methane and carbon monoxide emitted by human activities are present at background levels in the air over the ECE region and contribute to the formation of episodic peak ozone levels; that, in addition, their global-scale oxidation in the presence of nitrogen oxides contributes to the formation of the background levels of tropospheric ozone upon which photochemical episodes are superimposed; and that methane is expected to become the subject of control actions in other forums,

Recalling that the Executive Body for the Convention identified at its sixth session the need to control emissions of VOCs or their transboundary fluxes, as well as to control the incidence of photochemical oxidants, and the need for Parties that had already reduced these emissions to maintain and review their emission standards for VOCs,

Acknowledging the measures already taken by some Parties which have had the effect of reducing their national annual emissions of nitrogen oxides and VOCs,

Noting that some Parties have set air quality standards and/or objectives for tropospheric ozone and that standards for tropospheric ozone concentrations have been set by the World Health Organization and other competent bodies,

Determined to take effective action to control and reduce national annual emissions of VOCs or the transboundary fluxes of VOCs and the resulting secondary photochemical oxidant products, in particular by applying appropriate national or international emission standards to new mobile and new stationary sources and retrofitting existing major stationary sources, and also by limiting the content of components in products for industrial and domestic use that have the potential to emit VOCs,

Conscious that volatile organic compounds differ greatly from each other in their reactivity and in their potential to create tropospheric ozone and other photochemical oxidants and that, for any individual compounds, potential may vary from time to time and from place to place depending on meteorological and other factors,

Recognizing that such differences and variations should be taken into consideration if action to control and reduce emissions and transboundary fluxes of VOCs is to be as effective as possible in minimizing the formation of tropospheric ozone and other photochemical oxidants,

Taking into consideration existing scientific and technical data on emissions, atmospheric movements and effects on the environment of VOCs and photochemical oxidants, as well as on control technologies,

Recognizing that scientific and technical knowledge of these matters is developing and that it will be necessary to take such developments into account when reviewing the operation of the present Protocol and deciding on further action,

Noting that the elaboration of an approach based on critical levels is aimed at the establishment of an effect-oriented scientific basis to be taken into account when reviewing the operation of the present Protocol, and at deciding on further internationally agreed measures to limit and reduce emissions of VOCs or the transboundary fluxes of VOCs and photochemical oxidants,

Have agreed as follows:

Article 1

Definitions

For the purposes of the present Protocol,

1. "Convention" means the Convention on Long-range Transboundary Air Pollution, adopted in Geneva on 13 November 1979;

2. "EMEP" means the Cooperative Programme for Monitoring and Evaluation of the Long-range Transmission of Air Pollutants in Europe;

3. "Executive Body" means the Executive Body for the Convention constituted under article 10, paragraph 1, of the Convention;

4. "Geographical scope of EMEP" means the area defined in article 1, paragraph 4, of the Protocol to the 1979 Convention on Long-range Transboundary Air Pollution on Long-term Financing of the Cooperative Programme for Monitoring and Evaluation of the Long-range Transmission of Air Pollutants in Europe (EMEP), adopted in Geneva on 28 September 1984;

5. "Tropospheric ozone management area" (TOMA) means an area specified in annex I under conditions laid down in article 2, paragraph 2 (b);

6. "Parties" means, unless the context otherwise requires, the Parties to the present Protocol;

7. "Commission" means the United Nations Economic Commission for Europe;

8. "Critical levels" means concentrations of pollutants in the atmosphere for a specified exposure time below which direct adverse effects on receptors, such as human beings, plants, ecosystems or materials do not occur according to present knowledge;

9. "Volatile organic compounds", or "VOCs", means, unless otherwise specified, all organic compounds of anthropogenic nature, other than methane, that are capable of producing photochemical oxidants by reactions with nitrogen oxides in the presence of sunlight;

10. "Major source category" means any category of sources which emit air pollutants in the form of VOCs, including the categories described in annexes II and III, and which contribute at least 1 per cent of the total national emissions of VOCs on an annual basis, as measured or calculated in the first calendar year after the date of entry into force of the present Protocol, and every fourth year thereafter;

11. "New stationary source" means any stationary source of which the construction or substantial modification is commenced after the expiry of two years from the date of entry into force of the present Protocol;

12. "New mobile source" means any on-road motor vehicle which is manufactured after the expiry of two years from the date of entry into force of the present Protocol;

13. "Photochemical ozone creation potential" (POCP) means the potential of an individual VOC, relative to that of other VOCs, to form ozone by reaction with oxides of nitrogen in the presence of sunlight, as described in annex IV.

Article 2

Basic obligations

1. The Parties shall control and reduce their emissions of VOCs in order to reduce their transboundary fluxes and the fluxes of the resulting secondary photochemical oxidant products so as to protect human health and the environment from adverse effects.

2. Each Party shall, in order to meet the requirements of paragraph 1 above, control and reduce its national annual emissions of VOCs or their transboundary fluxes in any one of the following ways to be specified upon signature:

(a) It shall, as soon as possible and as a first step, take effective measures to reduce its national annual emissions of VOCs by at least 30 per cent by the year 1999, using 1988 levels as a basis or any other annual level during the period 1984 to 1990, which it may specify upon signature of or accession to the present Protocol; or

(b) Where its annual emissions contribute to tropospheric ozone concentrations in areas under the jurisdiction of one or more other Parties, and such emissions originate only from areas under its jurisdiction that are specified as TOMAs in annex I, it shall, as soon as possible and as a first step, take effective measures to:

(i) Reduce its annual emissions of VOCs from the areas so specified by at least 30 per cent by the year 1999, using 1988 levels as a basis or any other annual level during the period 1984-1990, which it may specify upon signature of or accession to the present Protocol; and

(ii) Ensure that its total national annual emissions of VOCs by the year 1999 do not exceed the 1988 levels; or

(c) Where its national annual emissions of VOCs were in 1988 lower than 500,000 tonnes and 20 kg/inhabitant and 5 tonnes/km^2, it shall, as soon as possible and as a first step, take effective measures to ensure at least that at the latest by the year 1999 its national annual emissions of VOCs do not exceed the 1988 levels.

3. (a) Furthermore, no later than two years after the date of entry into force of the present Protocol, each Party shall:

(i) Apply appropriate national or international emission standards to new stationary sources based on the best available technologies which are economically feasible, taking into consideration annex II;

(ii) Apply national or international measures to products that contain solvents and promote the use of products that are low in or do not contain VOCs, taking into consideration annex II, including the labelling of products specifying their VOC content;

(iii) Apply appropriate national or international emission standards to new mobile sources based on the best available technologies which are economically feasible, taking into consideration annex III; and

(iv) Foster public participation in emission control programmes through public announcements, encouraging the best use of all modes of transportation and promoting traffic management schemes.

(b) Furthermore, no later than five years after the date of entry into force of the present Protocol, in those areas in which national or international tropospheric ozone standards are exceeded or where transboundary fluxes originate or are expected to originate, each Party shall:

(i) Apply the best available technologies that are economically feasible to existing stationary sources in major source categories, taking into consideration annex II;

(ii) Apply techniques to reduce VOC emissions from petrol distribution and motor vehicle refuelling operations, and to reduce volatility of petrol, taking into consideration annexes II and III.

4. In carrying out their obligations under this article, Parties are invited to give highest priority to reduction and control of emissions of substances with the greatest POCP, taking into consideration the information contained in annex IV.

5. In implementing the present Protocol, and in particular any product substitution measures, Parties shall take appropriate steps to ensure that toxic and carcinogenic VOCs, and those that harm the stratospheric ozone layer, are not substituted for other VOCs.

6. The Parties shall, as a second step, commence negotiations, no later than six months after the date of entry into force of the present Protocol, on further steps to reduce national annual emissions of volatile organic compounds or transboundary fluxes of such emissions and their resulting secondary photochemical oxidant products, taking into account the best available scientific and technological developments, scientifically determined critical levels and internationally accepted target levels, the role of nitrogen oxides in the formation of photochemical oxidants and other elements resulting from the work programme undertaken under article 5.

7. To this end, the Parties shall cooperate in order to establish:

(a) More detailed information on the individual VOCs and their POCP values;

(b) Critical levels for photochemical oxidants;

(c) Reductions in national annual emissions or transboundary fluxes of VOCs and their resulting secondary photochemical oxidant products, especially as required to achieve agreed objectives based on critical levels;

(d) Control strategies, such as economic instruments, to obtain overall cost-effectiveness to achieve agreed objectives;

(e) Measures and a timetable commencing no later than 1 January 2000 for achieving such reductions.

8. In the course of these negotiations, the Parties shall consider whether it would be appropriate for the purposes specified in paragraph 1 to supplement such further steps with measures to reduce methane.

Article 3

FURTHER MEASURES

1. Measures required by the present Protocol shall not relieve Parties from their other obligations to take measures to reduce total gaseous emissions that may contribute significantly to climate change, to the formation of tropospheric background ozone or to the depletion of stratospheric ozone, or that are toxic or carcinogenic.

2. Parties may take more stringent measures than those required by the present Protocol.

3. The Parties shall establish a mechanism for monitoring compliance with the present Protocol. As a first step based on information provided pursuant to article 8 or other information, any Party which has reason to believe that another Party is acting or has acted in a manner inconsistent with its obligations under this Protocol may inform the Executive Body to that effect and, simultaneously, the Parties concerned. At the request of any Party, the matter may be taken up at the next meeting of the Executive Body.

Article 4

EXCHANGE OF TECHNOLOGY

1. The Parties shall, consistent with their national laws, regulations and practices, facilitate the exchange of technology to reduce emissions of VOCs, particularly through the promotion of:

(a) The commercial exchange of available technology;

(b) Direct industrial contacts and cooperation, including joint ventures;

(c) The exchange of information and experience;

(d) The provision of technical assistance.

2. In promoting the activities specified in paragraph 1 of this article, the Parties shall create favourable conditions by facilitating contacts and cooperation among appropriate organizations and individuals in the private and public sectors that are capable of providing technology, design and engineering services, equipment or finance.

3. The Parties shall, no later than six months after the date of entry into force of the present Protocol, com-

mence consideration of procedures to create more fa-vourable conditions for the exchange of technology to reduce emissions of VOCs.

Article 5

RESEARCH AND MONITORING TO BE UNDERTAKEN

The Parties shall give high priority to research and monitoring related to the development and application of methods to achieve national or international tropospheric ozone standards and other goals to protect human health and the environment. The Parties shall, in particular, through national or international research programmes, in the work-plan of the Executive Body and through other cooperative programmes within the framework of the Convention, seek to:

(a) Identify and quantify effects of emissions of VOCs, both anthropogenic and biogenic, and photo-chemical oxidants on human health, the environment and materials;

(b) Determine the geographical distribution of sensi-tive areas;

(c) Develop emission and air quality monitoring and model calculations including methodologies for the cal-culation of emissions, taking into account, as far as pos-sible, the different VOC species, both anthropogenic and biogenic, and their reactivity, to quantify the long-range transport of VOCs, both anthropogenic and biogenic, and related pollutants involved in the formation of pho-tochemical oxidants;

(d) Improve estimates of the performance and costs of technologies for control of emissions of VOCs and re-cord the development of improved and new technolo-gies;

(e) Develop, within the context of the approach based on critical levels, methods to integrate scientific, technical and economic data in order to determine appro-priate rational strategies for limiting VOC emissions and obtain overall cost-effectiveness to achieve agreed ob-jectives;

(f) Improve the accuracy of inventories of emissions of VOCs, both anthropogenic and biogenic, and harmo-nize the methods of their calculation or estimation;

(g) Improve their understanding of the chemical processes involved in the creation of photochemical oxi-dants;

(h) Identify possible measures to reduce emissions of methane.

Article 6

REVIEW PROCESS

1.   The Parties shall regularly review the present Protocol, taking into account the best available scientific substantiation and technological development.

2.   The first review shall take place no later than one year after the date of entry into force of the present Pro-tocol.

Article 7

NATIONAL PROGRAMMES, POLICIES AND STRATEGIES

The Parties shall develop without undue delay na-tional programmes, policies and strategies to implement the obligations under the present Protocol that shall serve as a means of controlling and reducing emissions of VOCs or their transboundary fluxes.

Article 8

INFORMATION EXCHANGE AND ANNUAL REPORTING

1.   The Parties shall exchange information by notify-ing the Executive Body of the national programmes, policies and strategies that they develop in accordance with article 7, and by reporting to it progress achieved under, and any changes to, those programmes, policies and strategies. In the first year after entry into force of this Protocol, each Party shall report on the level of emissions of VOCs in its territory and any TOMA in its territory, by total and, to the extent feasible, by sector of origin and by individual VOC, according to guidelines to be specified by the Executive Body for 1988 or any other year taken as the base year for article 2.2 and on the basis upon which these levels have been calculated.

2.   Furthermore each Party shall report annually:

(a) On the matters specified in paragraph 1 for the previous calendar year, and on any revision which may be necessary to the reports already made for earlier years;

(b) On progress in applying national or international emission standards and the control techniques required under article 2, paragraph 3;

(c) On measures taken to facilitate the exchange of technology.

3.   In addition, Parties within the geographical scope of EMEP shall report, at intervals to be specified by the Executive Body, information on VOC emissions by sec-tor of origin, with a spatial resolution, to be specified by the Executive Body, appropriate for purposes of model-ling the formation and transport of secondary photo-chemical oxidant products.

4.   Such information shall, as far as possible, be sub-mitted in accordance with a uniform reporting frame-work.

Article 9

CALCULATIONS

EMEP shall, utilizing appropriate models and measurements, provide to the annual meetings of the Executive Body relevant information on the long-range transport of ozone in Europe. In areas outside the geographical scope of EMEP, models appropriate to the particular circumstances of Parties to the Convention therein shall be used.

Article 10

ANNEXES

The annexes to the present Protocol shall form an integral part of the Protocol. Annex I is mandatory while annexes II, III and IV are recommendatory.

Article 11

AMENDMENTS TO THE PROTOCOL

1. Any Party may propose amendments to the present Protocol.

2. Proposed amendments shall be submitted in writing to the Executive Secretary of the Commission, who shall communicate them to all Parties. The Executive Body shall discuss the proposed amendments at its next annual meeting, provided that those proposals have been circulated by the Executive Secretary to the Parties at least 90 days in advance.

3. Amendments to the Protocol, other than amendments to its annexes, shall be adopted by consensus of the Parties present at a meeting of the Executive Body, and shall enter into force for the Parties which have accepted them on the ninetieth day after the date on which two-thirds of the Parties have deposited their instruments of acceptance thereof. Amendments shall enter into force for any Party which has accepted them after two-thirds of the Parties have deposited their instruments of acceptance of the amendment, on the ninetieth day after the date on which that Party deposited its instrument of acceptance of the amendments.

4. Amendments to the annexes shall be adopted by consensus of the Parties present at a meeting of the Executive Body and shall become effective 30 days after the date on which they have been communicated, in accordance with paragraph 5 of this article.

5. Amendments under paragraphs 3 and 4 of this article shall, as soon as possible after their adoption, be communicated by the Executive Secretary to all Parties.

Article 12

SETTLEMENT OF DISPUTES

If a dispute arises between two or more Parties as to the interpretation or application of the present Protocol, they shall seek a solution by negotiation or by any other method of dispute settlement acceptable to the parties to the dispute.

Article 13

SIGNATURE

1. The present Protocol shall be open for signature at Geneva from 18 November 1991 until 22 November 1991 inclusive, then at the United Nations Headquarters in New York until 22 May 1992, by the States members of the Commission as well as States having consultative status with the Commission, pursuant to paragraph 8 of Economic and Social Council resolution 36 (IV) of 28 March 1947, and by regional economic integration organizations, constituted by sovereign States members of the Commission, which have competence in respect of the negotiation, conclusion and application of international agreements in matters covered by the Protocol, provided that the States and organizations concerned are Parties to the Convention.

2. In matters within their competence, such regional economic integration organizations shall, on their own behalf, exercise the rights and fulfil the responsibilities which the present Protocol attributes to their member States. In such cases, the member States of these organizations shall not be entitled to exercise such rights individually.

Article 14

RATIFICATION, ACCEPTANCE, APPROVAL AND ACCESSION

1. The present Protocol shall be subject to ratification, acceptance or approval by Signatories.

2. The present Protocol shall be open for accession as from 22 May 1992 by the States and organizations referred to in article 13, paragraph 1.

Article 15

DEPOSITARY

The instruments of ratification, acceptance, approval or accession shall be deposited with the Secretary-General of the United Nations, who will perform the functions of Depositary.

Article 16

ENTRY INTO FORCE

1.   The present Protocol shall enter into force on the ninetieth day following the date on which the sixteenth instrument of ratification, acceptance, approval or accession has been deposited.

2.   For each State and organization referred to in article 13, paragraph 1, which ratifies, accepts or approves the present Protocol or accedes thereto after the deposit of the sixteenth instrument of ratification, acceptance, approval or accession, the Protocol shall enter into force on the ninetieth day following the date of deposit by such Party of its instrument of ratification, acceptance, approval or accession.

Article 17

WITHDRAWAL

At any time after five years from the date on which the present Protocol has come into force with respect to a Party, that Party may withdraw from it by giving written notification to the Depositary. Any such withdrawal shall take effect on the ninetieth day following the date of its receipt by the Depositary, or on such later date as may be specified in the notification of the withdrawal.

Article 18

AUTHENTIC TEXTS

The original of the present Protocol, of which the English, French and Russian texts are equally authentic, shall be deposited with the Secretary-General of the United Nations.

IN WITNESS WHEREOF the undersigned, being duly authorized thereto, have signed the present Protocol.

DONE at Geneva this eighteenth day of November one thousand nine hundred and ninety-one.

ANNEXES

ANNEX I

Designated tropospheric ozone management areas (TOMAs)

The following TOMAs are specified for the purposes of this Protocol:

Canada

TOMA No. 1: The Lower Fraser Valley in the Province of British Columbia.

This is a 16,800-km^2 area in the southwestern corner of the Province of British Columbia averaging 80 km in width and extending 200 km up the Fraser River Valley from the mouth of the river in the Strait of Georgia to Boothroyd, British Columbia. Its southern boundary is the Canada/United States international boundary and it includes the Greater Vancouver Regional District.

TOMA No. 2: The Windsor-Quebec Corridor in the Provinces of Ontario and Quebec.

This is a 157,000-km^2 area consisting of a strip of land 1,100 km long and averaging 140 km in width stretching from the City of Windsor (adjacent to Detroit in the United States) in the Province of Ontario to Quebec City in the Province of Quebec. The Windsor-Quebec Corridor TOMA is located along the north shore of the Great Lakes and the St. Lawrence River in Ontario and straddles the St. Lawrence River from the Ontario-Quebec border to Quebec City in Quebec. It includes the urban centres of Windsor, London, Hamilton, Toronto, Ottawa, Montreal, Trois-Rivières and Quebec City.

Norway

The total Norwegian mainland as well as the exclusive economic zone south of 62°N latitude in the region of the Economic Commission for Europe (ECE), covering an area of 466,000 km^2.

ANNEX II

Control measures for emissions of volatile organic compounds (VOCs) from stationary sources

Introduction

1. The aim of this annex is to provide the Parties to the Convention with guidance in identifying best available technologies to enable them to meet the obligations of the Protocol.

2. Information regarding emission performance and costs is based on official documentation of the Executive Body and its subsidiary bodies, in particular documents received and reviewed by the Task Force on Emissions of VOCs from Stationary Sources. Unless otherwise indicated, the techniques listed are considered to be well established on the basis of operational experience.

3. Experience with new products and new plants incorporating low-emission techniques, as well as with the retrofitting of existing plants, is continuously growing; the regular elaboration and amendment of the annex will therefore be necessary. Best available technologies identified for new plants can be applied to existing plants after an adequate transition period.

4. The annex lists a number of measures spanning a range of costs and efficiencies. The choice of measures for any particular case will depend on a number of factors, including economic circumstances, technological infrastructure and any existing VOC control implemented.

5. This annex does not, in general, take into account the specific species of VOC emitted by the different sources, but deals with best available technologies for VOC reduction. When measures are planned for some sources, it is worthwhile to consider giving priority to those activities which emit reactive rather than non-reactive VOCs (e.g. in the solvent-using sector). However, when such compound-specific measures are designed, other effects on the environment (e.g. global climate change) and on human health should also be taken into account.

45

I.   Major sources of VOC emissions from stationary sources

6. The major sources of anthropogenic non-methane VOC emissions from stationary sources are the following:

(a) Use of solvents;

(b) Petroleum industry including petroleum-product handling;

(c) Organic chemical industry;

(d) Small-scale combustion sources (e.g. domestic heating and small industrial boilers);

(e) Food industry;

(f) Iron and steel industry;

(g) Handling and treatment of wastes;

(h) Agriculture.

7. The order of the list reflects the general importance of the sources subject to the uncertainties of emission inventories. The distribution of VOC emissions according to different sources depends greatly on the fields of activity within the territory of any particular Party.

II.   General options for VOC-emission reduction

8. There are several possibilities for the control or prevention of VOC emissions. Measures for the reduction of VOC emissions focus on products and/or process modifications (including maintenance and operational control) and on the retrofitting of existing plants. The following list gives a general outline of measures available, which may be implemented either singly or in combination:

(a) Substitution of VOCs; e.g. the use of water-based degreasing baths, and paints, inks, glues or adhesives which are low in or do not contain VOCs;

(b) Reduction by best management practices such as good housekeeping, preventive maintenance programmes, or by changes in processes such as closed systems during utilization, storage and distribution of low-boiling organic liquids;

(c) Recycling and/or recovery of efficiently collected VOCs by control techniques such as adsorption, absorption, condensation and membrane processes; ideally, organic compounds can be reused on-site;

(d) Destruction of efficiently collected VOCs by control techniques such as thermal or catalytic incineration or biological treatment.

9. The monitoring of abatement procedures is necessary to ensure that appropriate control measures and practices are properly implemented for an effective reduction of VOC emissions. Monitoring of abatement procedures will include:

(a) The development of an inventory of those VOC-emission reduction measures, identified above, that have already been implemented;

(b) The characterization and quantification of VOC emissions from relevant sources by instrumental or other techniques;

(c) Periodic auditing of abatement measures implemented to ensure their continued efficient operation;

(d) Regularly scheduled reporting on (a), (b) and (c), using harmonized procedures, to regulatory authorities;

(e) Comparison, with the objectives of the Protocol, of VOC-emission reductions achieved in practice.

10. The investment/cost figures have been collected from various sources. On account of the many influencing factors, investment/cost figures are highly case-specific. If the unit "cost per tonne of VOC abated" is used for cost-efficient strategy considerations, it must be borne in mind that such specific figures are highly dependent on factors such as plant capacity, removal efficiency and raw gas VOC concentration, type of technology, and the choice of new installations as opposed to retrofitting. Illustrative cost figures should also be based on process-specific parameters, e.g. mg/m^2 treated (paints), kg/m^3 product or kg/unit.

11. Cost-efficient strategy considerations should be based on total costs per year (including capital and operational costs). VOC-emission reduction costs should also be considered within the framework of the overall process economics, e.g. the impact of control measures and costs on the costs of production.

III.   Control techniques

12. The major categories of available control techniques for VOC abatement are summarized in table 1. Those techniques chosen for inclusion in the table have been successfully applied commercially and are now well established. For the most part, they have been applied generally across sectors.

13. Sector-specific techniques, including the limitation of the solvent content of products, are given in sections IV and V.

14. Care should be taken to ensure that the implementation of these control techniques does not create other environmental problems. If incineration has to be used, it should be combined with energy recovery, where appropriate.

15. Using such techniques, concentrations of below 150 mg/m^3 (as total carbon, standard conditions) can usually be achieved in exhaust air flows. In most cases, emission values of 10-50 mg/m^3 can be achieved.

16. Another common procedure for destroying non-halogenated VOCs is to use VOC-laden gas streams as secondary air or fuel in existing energy-conversion units. However, this usually requires site-specific process modifications and therefore it too is excluded from the following table.

17. Data on efficiency are derived from operational experience and are considered to reflect the capabilities of current installations.

TABLE 1

A summary of available VOC control techniques, their efficiencies and costs

Technique	Lower concentration in air flow		Higher concentration in air flow		Application
	Efficiency	Cost	Efficiency	Cost	
Thermal incineration**	High	High	High	Medium	Wide for high concentration flows
Catalytic incineration**	High	Medium	Medium	Medium	More specialized for lower concentration flows
Adsorption* (activated carbon filters)	High	High	Medium	Medium	Wide for low concentration flows
Absorption (waste gas washing)	–	–	High	Medium	Wide for high concentration flows
Condensation*	–	–	Medium	Low	Special cases of high concentration flows only
Biofiltration	Medium to High	Low	Low***	Low	Mainly in low concentration flows, including odour control

Concentration:	Lower	< 3 g/m^3 (in many cases < 1 g/m^3)
	Higher	> 5 g/m^3
Efficiency:	High	$> 95\%$
	Medium	80-95%
	Low	$< 80\%$
Total cost:	High	> 500 ECU/t VOC abated
	Medium	150-500 ECU/t VOC abated
	Low	< 150 ECU/t VOC abated

* These processes can be combined with solvent recovery systems. Cost savings then ensue.

** Savings due to energy recovery are not included; these can reduce the costs considerably.

*** With buffering filters to dampen emission peaks, medium to high efficiencies are achieved at medium to low costs.

18. Cost data are more subject to uncertainty due to interpretation of costs, accountancy practices and site-specific conditions. Therefore the data provided are case-specific. They cover the cost ranges for the different techniques. The costs do, however, accurately reflect the relationships between the costs of the different techniques. Differences in costs between new and retrofit applications may in some cases be significant but do not differ sufficiently to change the order in table 1.

19. The choice of a control technique will depend on parameters such as the concentration of VOCs in the raw gas, gas volume flow, the type of VOCs, and others. Therefore, some overlap in the fields of application may occur; in that case, the most appropriate technique must be selected according to case-specific conditions.

IV. SECTORS

20. In this section, each VOC-emitting sector is characterized by a table containing the main emission sources, control measures including the best available technologies, their specific reduction efficiency and the related costs.

21. An estimate is also provided of the overall potential within each sector for reducing its VOC emissions. The maximum reduction potential refers to situations in which only a low level of control is in place.

22. Process-specific reduction efficiencies should not be confused with the figures given for the reduction potential of each sector. The former are technical feasibilities, while the latter take into account the likely penetration and other factors affecting each sector. The process-specific efficiencies are given only qualitatively, as follows:

$$I = > 95\%; \qquad II = 80\text{-}95\%; \qquad III = < 80\%$$

23. Costs depend on capacity, site-specific factors, accountancy practices and other factors. Consequently, costs may vary greatly; therefore, only qualitative information (medium, low, high) is provided, referring to comparisons of costs of different technologies mentioned for specific applications.

A. Industrial use of solvents

24. The industrial use of solvents is in many countries the biggest contributor to VOC emissions from stationary sources. Main sectors and control measures, including best available technologies and reduction efficiencies, are listed in table 2, and the best available technology is specified for each sector. There may be differences between small and large or new and old plants. For this reason, the estimated overall reduction potential quoted is below the values implied in table 2. The estimated overall reduction potential for this sector is up to 60 per cent. A further step to reduce episodic ozone formation potential can include the reformulation of the remaining solvents.

25. With respect to the industrial use of solvents, three approaches can in principle be used: a product-oriented approach which, for instance, leads to a reformulation of the product (paint, degreasing products, etc.); process-oriented changes; and add-on control technologies. For some industrial uses of solvents only a product-oriented approach is available (in the case of painting constructions, painting buildings, the industrial use of cleaning products, etc.). In all other cases, the product-oriented approach deserves priority, *inter alia*,

TABLE 2

VOC-emission control measures, reduction efficiency and costs for the solvent-using sector

Source of emission	Emission control measures	Reduction efficiency	Abatement costs and savings
Industrial surface coating	Conversion to:		
	powder paints	I	Savings
	low in/not containing VOCs	I-III	Low costs
	high solids	I-III	Savings
	Incineration:	I-II	Medium to high costs
	thermal	I-II	Medium costs
	catalytic	I-II	Medium costs
	Activated carbon adsorption		
Paper surface coating	Incinerator	I-II	Medium costs
	Radiation cure/waterborne inks	I-III	Low costs
Car manufacturing	Conversion to:	I	
	powder paints		
	water-based systems	I-II	Low costs
	high solid coating	II	
	Activated carbon adsorption	I-II	Low costs
	Incineration with heat recovery:		
	thermal	I-II	
	catalytic	I-II	
Commercial painting	Low in/not containing VOCs	I-II	Medium costs
	Low in/not containing VOCs	II-III	Medium costs
Printing	Low-solvent/water-based inks	II-III	Medium costs
	Letterpress: radiation cure	I	Low costs
	Activated carbon adsorption	I-II	High costs
	Absorption		
	Incineration:	I-II	
	thermal		
	catalytic		
	Biofiltration including buffer filter	I	Medium costs
Metal degreasing	Change-over to systems low in/not containing VOCs	I	
	Closed machines		
	Activated carbon adsorption	II	Low to high costs
	Cover, chilled freeboards	III	Low costs
Dry-cleaning	Recovery dryers and good housekeeping (closed cycles)	II-III	Low to medium costs
	Condensation	II	Low costs
	Activated carbon adsorption	II	Low costs
Flat wood panelling	Coatings low in/not containing VOCs	I	Low costs

I = > 95%;   II = 80-95%;   III = < 80%.

because of the positive spin-off effects on the solvent emission of the manufacturing industry. Furthermore, the environmental impact of emissions can be reduced by combining best available technology with product reformulation to replace solvents by less harmful alternatives. According to a combined approach of this kind, the maximum emission reduction potential of up to 60 per cent could lead to an improvement in environmental performance that is significantly higher.

26. There is rapid ongoing development towards low-solvent or solvent-free paints, which are among the most cost-effective solutions. For many plants, a combination of low-solvent and adsorption/incineration techniques are chosen. VOC-emission control for large-scale, industrial painting (e.g. of cars, domestic appliances) could be implemented relatively quickly. Emissions have been reduced as far as 60 g/m^2 in several countries. The technical possibility of reducing emissions from new plants to below 20 g/m^2 has been recognized by several countries.

27. For the degreasing of metal surfaces, alternative solutions are water-based treatment or closed machines with activated carbon for recovery, with low emissions.

28. For the different printing techniques, several methods to reduce VOC emissions are employed. These mainly involve the changing of inks, changes within the printing process using other printing methods, and gas cleaning techniques. Waterborne ink instead of solvent-based ink is used for flexographic printing on paper and is under development for printing on plastic. Waterborne inks for screen and rotogravure printing are available for some applications. The use of electron beam cured ink in offset eliminates VOCs and is used in the package printing industry. For some printing methods, UV-cured inks are available. Best available technology for publication rotogravure is the gas cleaning technique using carbon adsorbers. In packaging, the rotogravure recovery of solvent by adsorption (zeolites, active carbon) is practised, but incineration and absorption are also used. For heat-set, the web-offset thermal or catalytic incineration of exhaust gases is used. The incineration equipment often includes a unit for heat recovery.

29. For dry-cleaning, the best available technology consists of closed machines and treatment of the exhaust ventilation air by activated carbon filters.

B. *Petroleum industry*

30. The petroleum industry is one of the major contributors to VOC emissions from stationary sources. Emissions are from both refineries and distribution (including transportation and filling-stations). The following comments refer to table 3; the measures mentioned also include best available technology.

31. Refinery process emissions arise from fuel combustion, flaring of hydrocarbons, vacuum-system discharges and fugitive emissions from process units, such as flanges and connectors, opened lines and sampling systems. Other major VOC emissions within refineries and related activities result from storage, waste-water treatment processes, loading/discharging facilities such as harbours, truck- and railway-racks, pipeline terminals, and periodic operations such as shut-downs, servicing and start-ups (process-unit turnarounds).

32. Process-unit turnaround emissions may be controlled by venting vessel vapours to vapour recovery systems or controlled flaring.

33. Vacuum-system discharges may be controlled by condensation or by piping to boilers or heaters.

34. Fugitive emissions from process equipment in gas/vapour or light liquid service (e.g. automatic control valves, manual valves, pressure relief devices, sampling systems, pumps, compressors, flanges and connectors) can be reduced or prevented by regularly performing leak detection, repair programmes and preventive maintenance. Equipment with substantial leaks (e.g. valves, gaskets, seals, pumps, etc.) can be replaced by equipment that is more leakproof. For example, manual and automatic control valves can be changed for corresponding valves with bellow gaskets. Pumps in gas/vapour and light liquid service can be fitted with dual mechanical seals with controlled degassing vents. Compressors can be equipped with seals with a barrier fluid system that prevents leakage of the process fluid to the atmosphere, and leakage from compressors seals directed to the flares.

35. Pressure relief valves for media that may contain VOCs can be connected to a gas-collecting system and the gases collected burnt in process furnaces or flares.

36. VOC emissions from the storage of crude oil and products can be reduced by equipping fixed-roof tanks with internal floating roofs or by equipping floating-roof tanks with secondary seals.

37. VOC emissions from the storage of petrol and other light liquid components can be reduced by several means. Fixed-roof tanks can be equipped with internal floating roofs with primary and secondary seals or connected to a closed vent system and an effective control device, e.g. vapour recovery, flaring or combustion in process heaters. External floating-roof tanks with primary seals can be equipped with secondary seals, and/or supplemented with tight, fixed roofs, with pressure relief valves which can be connected to the flare.

38. VOC emissions in connection with waste-water handling and treatment can be reduced by several means. Water-seal controls can be installed, as can junction boxes, equipped with tight-fitting covers, in drain systems. Sewer lines can be covered. Alternatively, the drain system can be completely closed to the atmosphere. Oil-water separators, including separation tanks, skimmers, weirs, grit chambers, sludge hoppers and slop-oil facilities, can be equipped with fixed roofs and closed vent systems that direct vapours to a control de-

TABLE 3

VOC-emission control measures, reduction efficiency and costs for the petroleum industry

Source of emission	Emission control measures	Reduction efficiency	Abatement costs and savings
Petroleum refineries			
Fugitive emissions	Regular inspection and maintenance	III	Medium costs
Process-unit turnarounds	Flares/process furnace vapour recovery	I	Not available
Waste-water separator	Floating cover	II	Medium costs/savings
Vacuum process system	Surface contact condensors	I	
	Non-condensable VOCs piped to heaters or furnaces		
Incineration of sludge	Thermal incineration	I	
Storage of crude oil and products			
Petrol	Internal floating roofs with secondary seals	I - II	Savings
	Floating roof tanks with secondary seals	II	Savings
Crude oil	Floating roof tanks with secondary seals	II	Savings
Petrol marketing terminals (loading and unloading of trucks, barges and trains)	Vapour recovery unit	I - II	Savings
Petrol service stations	Vapour balance on tank trucks (Stage I)	I - II	Low costs/savings
	Vapour balance during refuelling (refuelling nozzles) (Stage II)	I(- II**)	Medium costs*

I = > 95%; II = 80-95%; III = < 80%.

* Depending on capacity (station size), retrofitting or new service stations.

** Will increase with increasing penetration of standardization of vehicle filling pipes.

vice, designed either for the recovery or destruction of the VOC vapours. Alternatively, oil-water separators can be equipped with floating roofs with primary and secondary seals. The effective reduction of VOC emissions from waste-water treatment plants can be achieved by draining oil from process equipment to the slop-oil system, thus minimizing the oil-flow into the waste-water treatment plant. The temperature of incoming water can also be controlled in order to lower emissions to the atmosphere.

39.   The petrol storage and distribution sector has a high reduction potential. Emission control covering the loading of petrol at the refinery (via intermediate terminals) up to its discharge at petrol service stations is defined as Stage I; control of emissions from the refuelling of cars at service stations is defined as Stage II (see para. 33 of annex III on Control measures for emissions of volatile organic compounds (VOCs) from on-road motor vehicles).

40.   Stage I control consists of vapour balancing and vapour collection at the loading of petrol, and recovering the vapour in recovery units. Furthermore, vapour collected at service stations from the discharge of petrol from trucks can be returned and recovered in vapour recovery units.

41.   Stage II control consists of vapour balancing between the vehicle fuel tank and the service station's underground storage tank.

42.   Stage II together with Stage I is the best available technology for reducing evaporative emissions during petrol distribution. A complementary means of re-

ducing VOC emissions from fuel storage and handling is to reduce fuel volatility.

43.   The overall reduction potential in the petroleum industry sector is up to 80 per cent. This maximum could be reached only where the current level of emission control is low.

C.   *Organic chemical industry*

44.   The chemical industry also makes a considerable contribution to VOC emissions from stationary sources. The emissions are of different characters with a wide range of pollutants, because of the variety of products and production processes. Process emissions can be divided into the following major subcategories: reactor-process emissions, air-oxidation emissions and distillation, and other separation processes. Other significant emission sources are from leaks, storage and product transfer (loading/unloading).

45.   For new plants, process modifications and/or new processes often reduce emissions considerably. So-called "add-on" or "end-of-pipe" techniques such as adsorption, absorption, thermal and catalytic incineration in many cases represent alternative or complementary technologies. To reduce evaporation losses from storage tanks and emissions from loading and unloading facilities, the control measures recommended for the petroleum industry (table 3) can be applied. Control measures including best available technologies and their process-related reduction efficiencies are given in table 4.

TABLE 4

VOC-emission control measures, reduction efficiency and costs for the organic chemical industry

Source of emission	*Emission control measures*		*Reduction efficiency*	*Abatement costs and savings*
Fugitive emissions	Leak detection and repair programme – regular inspection		III	Low costs
Storage and handling	– See table 3 –			
Process emissions	General measures: – carbon adsorption		I - II	n.a.
	– incineration:	– thermal	I - II	Medium to high costs
		– catalytic	I - II	n.a.
	– absorption			n.a.
	– biofiltration		n.a.	n.a.
	– flaring			
– Formaldehyde production	– incineration:	– thermal	I	High costs
		– catalytic	I	
– Polyethylene production	– flaring		I	Medium costs
	– catalytic incineration		I - II	
– Polystyrene production	– thermal incineration		I	Medium costs
	– flaring			
– Vinyl chloride production	Process modifications (examples): – substitution of air by oxygen in the oxychlorination step		II	n.a.
	– flaring		I	Medium costs
– Polyvinylchloride production	– slurry stripping of monomer		II	n.a.
	– Nitro-2-methyl-1-propanol-1 absorption		I	Savings
– Polypropylene production	– high yield catalyst		I	n.a.
– Ethylene oxide production	– substitution of air by oxygen		I	n.a.

n.a.: not available.
I = > 95%;   II = 80-95%;   III = < 80%.

46.   The feasible overall reduction potential in the organic chemical industry is up to 70 per cent, depending on the industry mix and the extent to which control technologies and practices are in place.

D.   *Stationary combustion*

47.   Optimal VOC-emission reduction from stationary combustion depends on the efficient use of fuel at the national level (table 5). It is also important to ensure the effective combustion of fuel by the use of good operational procedures, efficient combustion appliances and advanced combustion-management systems.

TABLE 5

VOC-emission control measures for stationary combustion sources

Source of emission	Emission control measures
Small-scale combustion sources	Energy savings, e.g. insulation Regular inspection Replacement of old furnaces Natural gas and fuel oil instead of solid fuels Central heating system District heating system
Industrial and commercial sources	Energy savings Better maintenance Fuel-type modification Change of furnace and load Change of burning conditions
Stationary internal combustion sources	Catalytic converters Thermal reactors

48.   For small systems in particular, there is still a considerable reduction potential, especially in the burning of solid fuels. VOC reduction in general is achievable by the replacement of old stoves/boilers and/or fuel-switching to gas. The replacement of single room stoves by central heating systems and/or the replacement of individual heating systems in general reduces pollution; however, overall energy efficiency has to be taken into account. Fuel-switching to gas is a very effective control measure, provided the distribution system is leakproof.

49.   For most countries, the VOC-reduction potential for power plants is negligible. On account of the uncertain replacement/fuel-switch involved, no figures can be given regarding the overall reduction potential and the related costs.

E.   *Food industry*

50.   The food industry sector covers a wide range of VOC-emitting processes from large and small plants (table 6). The major sources of VOC emissions are:

(a) Production of alcoholic beverages;

(b) Baking;

(c) Vegetable oil extraction using mineral oils;

(d) Animal rendering.

Alcohol is the principal VOC from (a) and (b). Aliphatic hydrocarbons are the principal VOC from (c).

51.   Other potential sources include:

(a) Sugar industry and sugar use;

(b) Coffee and nut roasting;

(c) Frying (chipped potatoes, crisps, etc.);

(d) Fish meal processing;

(e) Preparation of cooked meats, etc.

52.   VOC emissions are typically odorous, of low concentration with high volume flow and water content. For this reason, the use of biofilters has been used as an abatement technique. Conventional techniques such as absorption, adsorption, thermal and catalytic incineration have also been used. The principal advantage of biofilters is their low operational cost compared with other techniques. Nevertheless, periodic maintenance is required.

53.   It may be feasible for larger fermentation plants and bakeries to recover alcohol by condensation.

54.   Aliphatic hydrocarbon emissions from oil extraction are minimized by using closed cycles and good housekeeping to prevent losses from valves and seals, etc. Different oil seeds require different volumes of min-

TABLE 6

VOC-emission control measures, reduction efficiency and costs for the food industry

Source of emission	Emission control measures	Reduction efficiency	Abatement costs
In general	Closed cycles Bio-oxidation Condensation and treatment Adsorption/absorption Thermal/catalytic incineration	 II I	 Low* High
Vegetable-oil processing	Process-integrated measures Adsorption Membrane technique Incineration in process furnace	III	Low
Animal rendering	Biofiltration	II	Low*

* Owing to the fact that these processes are usually applied to gases with low VOC concentrations, the costs per cubic metre of gas are low, although VOC abatement per tonne is high.

I = > 95%;   II = 80-95%;   III = < 80%.

eral oil for extraction. Olive oil can be extracted mechanically, in which case no mineral oil is necessary.

55. The technologically feasible overall reduction potential in the food industry is estimated to be up to 35 per cent.

F. *Iron and steel industry (including ferro-alloys, casting, etc.)*

56. In the iron and steel industry, VOC emissions may be from a variety of sources:

(*a*) Processing of input materials (cokeries; agglomeration plants: sintering, pelletizing, briquetting; scrap-handling);

(*b*) Metallurgical reactors (submerged arc furnaces; electric arc furnaces; converters, especially if using scrap; (open) cupolas; blast furnaces);

(*c*) Product handling (casting; reheating furnaces; and rolling mills).

57. Reducing the carbon carrier in raw materials (e.g. on sintering belts) reduces the potential of VOC emissions.

58. In the case of open metallurgical reactors, VOC emissions may occur especially from contaminated scrap and under pyrolytic conditions. Special attention has to be paid to the collection of gases from charging and tapping operations, in order to minimize fugitive VOC emissions.

59. Special attention has to be paid to scrap which is contaminated by oil, grease, paint, etc., and to the separation of fluff (non-metallic parts) from metallic scrap.

60. The processing of products usually entails fugitive emissions. In the case of casting, emissions of pyrolysis gases occur, chiefly from organically bonded sands. These emissions can be reduced by choosing low-emission bonding resins and/or minimizing the quantity of binders. Biofilters have been tested on such flue gases. Oil mist in the air from rolling mills can be reduced to low levels by filtration.

61. Coking plants are an important VOC emission source. Emissions arise from: coke oven gas leakage, the loss of VOCs normally diverted to an associated distillation plant, and from the combustion of coke oven gas and other fuel. VOC emissions are reduced mainly by the following measures: improved sealing between oven doors and frames and between charging holes and covers; maintaining suction from ovens even during charging; dry quenching either by direct cooling with inert gases or by indirect cooling with water; pushing directly into the dry quenching unit; and efficient hooding during pushing operations.

G. *Handling and treatment of waste*

62. Concerning municipal solid waste control, the primary objectives are to reduce the amount of waste produced and to reduce the amount to be treated. In addition, the waste treatment should be optimized from an environmental point of view.

63. If landfill processes are used, VOC-emission control measures for the treatment of municipal waste should be linked to an efficient collection of the gases (mostly methane).

64. These emissions can be destroyed (incineration). Another option is the purification of the gas (bio-oxidation, absorption, activated carbon, adsorption) leading to use of the gas for energy production.

65. The landfill of industrial waste containing VOCs leads to VOC emissions. This point has to be taken into account in the definition of waste-management policies.

66. The overall reduction potential is estimated to be 30 per cent, though this figure includes methane.

H. *Agriculture*

67. The principal sources of VOC emissions from agriculture are:

(*a*) Burning of agricultural waste, particularly straw and stubble;

(*b*) Use of organic solvents in pesticide formulations;

(*c*) Anaerobic degradation of animal feeds and wastes.

68. VOC emissions are reduced by:

(*a*) Controlled disposal of straw as opposed to the common practice of open-field burning;

(*b*) Minimal use of pesticides with high organic solvent contents, and/or the use of emulsions and water-based formulations;

(*c*) Composting of waste, combining manure with straw, etc.;

(*d*) Abatement of exhaust gases from animal houses, manure drying plant, etc., by use of biofilters, adsorption, etc.

69. In addition, alterations of feed reduce emissions of gas from animals, and the recovery of gases for use as fuel is a possibility.

70. It is not currently possible to estimate the reduction potential of VOC emissions from agriculture.

V. PRODUCTS

71. In circumstances in which abatement by control techniques is not appropriate, the sole means of reducing VOC emissions is by altering the composition of products used. The main sectors and products concerned are: adhesives used in households, light industry, shops and offices; paints for use in households; household cleaning and personal care products; office products such as correcting fluids and car maintenance products. In any other situation in which products like those mentioned above are used (e.g. painting, light industry), alterations in product composition are highly preferable.

72. Measures aimed at reducing VOC emissions from such products are:

(a) Product substitution;

(b) Product reformulation;

(c) Altering the packaging of products, especially for reformulated products.

73. Instruments designed to influence market choice include:

(a) Labelling to ensure that consumers are well informed of the VOC content;

(b) Active encouragement of low-VOC-content products (e.g. the "Blue Angel" scheme);

(c) Fiscal incentives linked to VOC content.

74. The efficiency of these measures depends on the VOC content of the products involved and the availability and acceptability of alternatives. Reformulation should be checked to ensure that products do not create problems elsewhere (e.g. increased emissions of chloro-fluorocarbons (CFCs)).

75. VOC-containing products are used for industrial as well as domestic purposes. In either case the use of low-solvent alternatives may entail changes in application equipment and in work practices.

76. Paints commonly used for industrial and domestic purposes have an average solvent content of about 25 to 60 per cent. For most applications, low-solvent or solvent-free alternatives are available or under development:

(a) Paint for use in the light industry:

Powder paint   = 0% VOC content in product

Waterborne paint = 10% VOC content in product

Low-solvent paint= 15% VOC content in product

(b) Paint for domestic use:

Waterborne paint = 10% VOC content in product

Low-solvent paint= 15% VOC content in product

Switching over to alternative paints is expected to result in an overall VOC-emission reduction of about 45 to 60 per cent.

77. Most adhesive products are used in industry, while domestic uses account for less than 10 per cent. About 25 per cent of the adhesives in use contain VOC solvents. For these adhesives, the solvent content varies widely and may constitute half the weight of the product. For several application areas, low-solvent/solvent-free alternatives are available. This source category therefore offers a high reduction potential.

78. Ink is mainly used for industrial printing processes, with solvent contents differing widely, up to 95 per cent. For most printing processes, low-solvent inks are available or under development in particular for printing on paper (see para. 28).

79. About 40 to 60 per cent of VOC emissions from consumer products (including office products and those used in car maintenance) are from aerosols. There are three basic ways of reducing VOC emissions from consumer products:

(a) Substitution of propellants and the use of mechanical pumps;

(b) Reformulation;

(c) Change of packaging.

80. The potential reduction of VOC emissions from consumer products is estimated to be 50 per cent.

Annex III

Control measures for emissions of volatile organic compounds (VOCs) from on-road motor vehicles

Introduction

1. This annex is based on information on emission control performance and costs contained in official documentation of the Executive Body and its subsidiary bodies; in the report on Volatile Organic Compounds from On-road Vehicles: Sources and Control Options, prepared for the Working Group on Volatile Organic Compounds; in documentation of the Inland Transport Committee of the Economic Commission for Europe (ECE) and its subsidiary bodies (in particular, documents TRANS/SC1/WP.29/R.242, 486 and 506); and on supplementary information provided by governmentally designated experts.

2. The regular elaboration and amendment of this annex will be necessary in the light of continuously expanding experience with new vehicles incorporating low-emission technology and the development of alternative fuels, as well as with retrofitting and other strategies for existing vehicles. The annex cannot be an exhaustive statement of technical options; its aim is to provide guidance to Parties in identifying economically feasible technologies for fulfilling their obligations under the Protocol. Until other data become available, this annex concentrates on on-road vehicles only.

I. MAJOR SOURCES OF VOC EMISSIONS FROM MOTOR VEHICLES

3. Sources of VOC emissions from motor vehicles have been divided into: (a) tailpipe emissions; (b) evaporative and refuelling emissions; and (c) crankcase emissions.

4. Road transport (excluding petrol distribution) is a major source of anthropogenic VOC emissions in most ECE countries and contributes between 30 and 45 per cent of total man-made VOC emissions in the ECE region as a whole. By far the largest source of road transport VOC emissions is the petrol-fuelled vehicle which accounts for 90 per cent of total traffic emissions of VOCs (of which 30 to 50 per cent are evaporative emissions). Evaporative and refuelling emissions result primarily from petrol use, and are considered very low in the case of diesel fuels.

II. GENERAL ASPECTS OF CONTROL TECHNOLOGIES FOR VOC EMISSIONS FROM ON-ROAD MOTOR VEHICLES

5. The motor vehicles considered in this annex are passenger cars, light-duty trucks, on-road heavy-duty vehicles, motor cycles and mopeds.

6. While this annex deals with both new and in-use vehicles, it is primarily focused on VOC-emission control for new vehicle types.

7. This annex also provides guidance on the influence of changes in petrol properties on evaporative VOC emissions. Fuel substitution (e.g. natural gas, liquefied petroleum gas (LPG), methanol) can also provide VOC-emission reductions but this is not considered in this annex.

8. Cost figures for the various technologies given are manufacturing cost estimates rather than retail prices.

9. It is important to ensure that vehicle designs are capable of meeting emission standards in service. This can be done through ensuring conformity of production, full useful-life durability, warranty of emission-control components, and recall of defective vehicles. For in-use vehicles, continued emission-control performance can also be ensured by an effective inspection and maintenance programme, and measures against tampering and misfuelling.

10. Emissions from in-use vehicles can be reduced through programmes such as fuel volatility controls, eco-

nomic incentives to encourage the accelerated introduction of desirable technology, low-level oxygenated fuel blends, and retrofitting. Fuel volatility control is the single most effective measure that can be taken to reduce VOC emissions from in-use motor vehicles.

11. Technologies that incorporate catalytic converters require the use of unleaded fuel. Unleaded petrol should therefore be generally available.

12. Measures to reduce VOC and other emissions by the management of urban and long-distance traffic, though not elaborated in this annex, are important as an efficient additional approach to reducing VOC emissions. Key measures for traffic management aim at improving the modal split through tactical, structural, financial and restrictive elements.

13. VOC emissions from uncontrolled motor vehicles contain significant levels of toxic compounds, some of which are known carcinogens. The application of VOC reduction technologies (tailpipe, evaporative, refuelling and crankcase) reduces these toxic emissions in generally the same proportion as the VOC reductions achieved. The level of toxic emissions can also be reduced by modifying certain fuel parameters (e.g. reducing benzene levels in petrol).

III. CONTROL TECHNOLOGIES FOR TAILPIPE EMISSIONS

(a) *Petrol-fuelled passenger cars and light-duty trucks*

14. The main technologies for controlling VOC emissions are listed in table 1.

15. The basis for comparison in table 1 is technology option B, representing non-catalytic technology designed in response to the requirements of the United States for 1973/1974 or of ECE regulation 15-04 pursuant to the 1958 Agreement concerning the Adoption of Uniform Conditions of Approval and Reciprocal Recognition of Approval for Motor Vehicle Equipment and Parts. The table also presents achievable emission levels for open- and closed-loop catalytic control as well as their cost implications.

TABLE 1

Tailpipe emission control technologies for petrol-fuelled passenger cars and light-duty trucks

		Emission level (%)		Cost*
	Technology option	*4-stroke*	*2-stroke*	*(US$)*
A.	Uncontrolled situation	400	900	—
B.	Engine modifications (engine design, carburation and ignition systems, air injection)	100 (1.8 g/km)	–	**
C.	Open-loop catalyst	50	–	150-200
D.	Closed-loop three-way catalyst	10-30	–	250-450***
E.	Advanced closed-loop three-way catalyst ..	6	–	350-600***

    * Additional production-cost estimates per vehicle, relative to technology option B.

    ** Costs for engine modifications from options A to B are estimated at US$ 40-100.

    *** Under technology options D and E, CO and NO_x emissions are also substantially reduced, in addition to VOC reductions. Technology options B and C can also result in some CO and/or NO_x control.

16. The "uncontrolled" level (A) in table 1 refers to the 1970 situation in the ECE region, but may still prevail in certain areas.

17. The emission level in table 1 reflects emissions measured using standard test procedures. Emissions from vehicles on the road may differ significantly because of the effect, *inter alia*, of ambient temperature, operating conditions, fuel properties, and maintenance. However, the reduction potential indicated in table 1 is considered representative of reductions achievable in use.

18. The best currently available technology is option D. This technology achieves large reductions of VOC, CO and NO_x emissions.

19. In response to regulatory programmes for further VOC emission reductions (e.g. in Canada and the United States), advanced closed-loop three-way catalytic converters are being developed (option E). These improvements will focus on more powerful engine-management controls, improved catalysts, on-board diagnostic systems (OBD) and other advances. These systems will become best available technology by the mid-1990s.

20. A special category are two-stroke engine cars which are used in parts of Europe; these cars currently have very high VOC emissions. Hydrocarbon emissions from two-stroke engines are typically between 45.0 and 75.0 grams per test, according to the European driving cycle. Attempts are under way to apply engine modifications and catalytic after-treatment to this type of engine. Data are needed on the reduction potentials and durability of these solutions. Furthermore, different two-stroke engine designs are currently being developed that have the potential for lower emissions.

(b) *Diesel-fuelled passenger cars and trucks*

21. Diesel-fuelled passenger cars and light-duty trucks have very low VOC emissions, generally lower than those resulting from closed-loop catalytic control on petrol-fuelled cars. However, their emissions of particulates and NO_x are higher.

22. No ECE country currently has rigorous tailpipe VOC control programmes for heavy-duty diesel-fuelled vehicles, because of their generally low VOC emission rates. However, many countries have diesel particulate control programmes, and the technology that is employed to control particulates (e.g. combustion chamber and injection system improvements) has the net end result of lowering VOC emissions as well.

23. Tailpipe VOC emission rates from heavy-duty diesel-fuelled vehicles are expected to be reduced by two thirds as the result of a vigorous particulate control programme.

24. VOC species emitted from diesel-fuelled engines are different from those emitted by petrol-fuelled engines.

(c) *Motor cycles and mopeds*

25. VOC emission control technologies for motor cycles are summarized in table 2. Current ECE regulations (R.40) can normally be met without requiring reduction technologies. The future standards of Austria and Switzerland may require oxidizing catalytic converters for two-stroke engines in particular.

26. For two-stroke mopeds with small oxidizing catalytic converters, a VOC-emission reduction of 90 per cent is achievable, at additional production costs of US$ 30-50. In Austria and Switzerland, standards requiring this technology are already in force.

IV. CONTROL TECHNOLOGIES FOR EVAPORATIVE AND REFUELLING EMISSIONS

27. *Evaporative emissions* consist of fuel vapour emitted from the engine and fuel system. They are divided into: (*a*) diurnal emissions, which result from the "breathing" of the fuel tank as it is heated and cooled over the course of a day; (*b*) hot-soak emissions produced by the heat from the engine after it is shut down; (*c*) running losses from the fuel system while the vehicle is in operation; and (*d*) resting losses such as from open-bottom canisters (where used) and from some plastic fuel-system materials which are reportedly subject to permeation losses, in which petrol slowly diffuses through the material.

28. The control technology typically used for evaporative emissions from petrol-fuelled vehicles includes a charcoal canister (and associated plumbing) and a purge system to burn the VOCs in a controlled manner in the engine.

TABLE 2

Tailpipe emission control technologies and performance for motor cycles

		Emission level (%)		Cost*
	Technology option	*2-stroke*	*4-stroke*	*(US$)*
A.	Uncontrolled	400	100	—
		(9.6 g/km)	(2 g/km)	—
B.	Best non-catalyst	200	60	—
C.	Oxidizing catalytic converter, secondary air	30-50	20	50
D.	Closed-loop three-way catalytic converter ..	not applicable	10**	350

* Additional production-cost estimates per vehicle.

** Expected to be available by 1991 for a few specific motor cycle types (prototypes already constructed and tested).

29.   Experience with existing evaporative-emission control programmes in the United States indicates that evaporative-emission control systems have not provided the degree of control desired, especially during severe ozone-prone days. This is partly because the volatility of in-use petrol is much higher than that of certification-test petrol. It is also due to an inadequate test procedure that resulted in inadequate control technology. The United States evaporative-emission control programme in the 1990s will emphasize reduced-volatility fuels for use in summer and an improved test procedure to encourage advanced evaporative control systems that will result in the in-use control of the four emission sources mentioned in paragraph 27 above. For countries with high volatility petrol, the single most cost-effective measure to reduce VOC emissions is to reduce volatility of in-use petrol.

30.   In general, effective evaporative-emission control requires the consideration of: (a) control of petrol volatility, adjusted to climatic conditions; and (b) an appropriate test procedure.

31.   A list of control options, reduction potentials and cost estimates is given in table 3, with option B as the best available control technology at present. Option C will soon become best available technology and will represent a significant improvement over option B.

32.   The fuel economy benefits associated with evaporative-emission controls are estimated at less than 2 per cent. The benefits are due to the higher energy density, and low Reid vapour pressure (RVP) of fuel, and to the combustion rather than venting of captured vapours.

33.   In principle, emissions that are released during refuelling of vehicles can be recovered by systems installed at petrol stations (Stage II) or by systems on board of vehicles. Controls at petrol stations are a well-established technology, while on-board systems have been demonstrated using several prototypes. The question of in-use safety of on-board vapour recovery systems is presently under study. It may be appropriate to develop safety performance standards in conjunction with on-board vapour recovery systems to assure their safe design. Stage II controls can be implemented more quickly since service stations in a given area can be fitted with these controls. Stage II controls benefit all petrol-fuelled vehicles while on-board systems only benefit new vehicles.

34.   While evaporative emissions from motor cycles and mopeds are at present uncontrolled in the ECE region, the same general control technologies as for petrol-fuelled cars can be applied.

TABLE 3

Evaporative-emission control measures and reduction potentials for petrol-fuelled passenger cars and light-duty trucks

	Technology option	VOC reduction potential (%)[1]	Cost (US$)[2]
A.	Small canister, lenient RVP[3] limits, 1980s US Test Procedure	< 80	20
B.	Small canister, stringent RVP limits,[4] 1980s US Test Procedure	80-95	20
C.	Advanced evaporative controls, stringent RVP limits,[4] 1990s US Test Procedure[5]	> 95	33

[1] Relative to uncontrolled situation.

[2] Additional production-cost estimates per vehicle.

[3] Reid vapour pressure.

[4] Based on United States data, assuming an RVP limit of 62 kPa during warm season at a cost of US$ 0.0038 per litre. Taking account of the fuel economy benefit associated with low RVP petrol, the adjusted cost estimate is US$ 0.0012 per litre.

[5] United States Test Procedure in the 1990s will be designed for the more effective control of multiple diurnal emissions, running losses, operation under high ambient temperature, hot-soak conditions following extended operation, and resting losses.

ANNEX IV

Classification of volatile organic compounds (VOCs) based on their photochemical ozone creation potential (POCP)

1. This annex summarizes the information available and identifies the still existing elements to develop in order to guide the work to be carried out. It is based on information regarding hydrocarbons and ozone formation contained in two notes prepared for the Working Group on Volatile Organic Compounds (EB.AIR/WG.4/R.11 and R.13/Rev.1); on the results of further research carried out, in particular in Austria, Canada, Germany, Netherlands, Sweden, the United Kingdom, the United States of America and the EMEP Meteorological Synthesizing Centre-West (MSC-W); and on supplementary information provided by governmentally designated experts.

2. The final aim of the POCP approach is to provide guidance on regional and national control policies for volatile organic compounds (VOCs), taking into account the impact of each VOC species as well as sectoral VOC emissions in episodic ozone formation expressed in terms of the photochemical ozone creation potential (POCP), which is defined as the change in photochemical ozone production due to a change in emission of that particular VOC. POCP may be determined by photochemical model calculations or by laboratory experiments. It serves to illustrate different aspects of episodic oxidant formation; e.g. peak ozone or accumulated ozone production during an episode.

3. The POCP concept is being introduced because there is a large variation between the importance of particular VOCs in the production of ozone during episodes. A fundamental feature of the concept is that, in the presence of sunlight and NO_x, each VOC produces ozone in a similar way despite large variations in the circumstances under which ozone is produced.

4. Different photochemical model calculations indicate that substantial reduction of VOCs and NO_x emissions are necessary (order of magnitude above 50 per cent in order to achieve significant ozone reduction). Moreover the maximum concentrations of ozone near the ground are reduced in a less than proportional way when VOC emissions are reduced. This effect is shown in principle by theoretical scenario calculation. When all species are reduced by the same proportion, maximum ozone values (above 75 ppb hourly average) in Europe are reduced depending on the existing ozone level by only 10-15 per cent if the mass of non-methane man-made VOC emissions is reduced by 50 per cent. By contrast, if emissions of the most important (in terms of POCP and mass values or reactivity) non-methane man-made VOC species were reduced by 50 per cent (by mass), the calculated result is a 20-30 per cent reduction of peak episodic ozone concentration. This confirms the merits of a POCP approach to determine priorities for VOC emission control and clearly shows that VOCs may at least be divided into large categories, according to their importance in episodic ozone formation.

5. POCP values and reactivity scales have been calculated as estimates, each based on a particular scenario (e.g. emission increases and decreases, air mass trajectories) and targeted towards a particular objective (e.g. peak ozone concentration, integrated ozone, average ozone). POCP values and reactivity scales are dependent on chemical mechanisms. Clearly there are differences between the different estimates of POCPs, which in some cases can span more than a factor of four. The POCP numbers are not constant but vary in space and time. To give an example: the calculated POCP of ortho-xylene in the so-called "France-Sweden" trajectory has a value of 41 on the first day and of 97 on the fifth day of the travelling time. According to calculations of the Meteorological Synthesizing Centre-West (MSC-W) of EMEP, the POCP of ortho-xylene for O_3 over 60 ppb, varies between 54 and 112 (5 to 95 percentiles) for the grids of the EMEP area. The variation of the POCP in time and space is not only caused by the VOC composition of the air parcel due to man-made emissions but is also a result of meteorological variations. The fact is that any reactive VOC can contribute to the episodical formation of photochemical oxidants to a higher or lower extent, depending on the concentrations of NO_x and VOC and meteorological parameters. Hydrocarbons with very low reactivity, like methane, methanol, ethane and some chlorinated hydrocarbons contribute in a negligible manner to this process. There are also differences as a result of meteorological variations between particular days and over Europe as a whole. POCP values are implicitly dependent on how emission inventories are calculated. Currently there is no consistent method or information available across Europe. Clearly, further work has to be done on the POCP approach.

6. Natural isoprene emissions from deciduous trees, together with nitrogen oxides (NO_x) mainly from man-made sources, can make a significant contribution to ozone formation in warm summer weather in areas with a large coverage of deciduous trees.

7. In table 1, VOC species are grouped according to their importance in the production of episodic peak ozone concentrations. Three groups have been selected. Importance in table 1 is expressed on the basis of VOC emission per unit mass. Some hydrocarbons, such as n-butane, become important because of their mass emission although they may not appear so according to their OH reactivity.

8. Tables 2 and 3 show the impacts of individual VOCs expressed as indices relative to the impact of a single species (ethylene) which is given an index of 100. They indicate how such indices, i.e. POCPs, may give guidance for assessing the impact of different VOC emission reductions.

9. Table 2 shows averaged POCPs for each major source category based on a central POCP estimate for

each VOC species in each source category. Emission inventories independently determined in the United Kingdom and Canada have been used in this compilation and presentation. For many sources, e.g. motor vehicles, combustion installations, and many industrial processes, mixtures of hydrocarbons are emitted. Measures to reduce specifically the VOC compounds identified in the POCP approach as very reactive are in most cases unavailable. In practice, most of the possible reduction measures will reduce emissions by mass irrespective of their POCPs.

10. Table 3 compares a number of different weighting schemes for a selected range of VOC species. In assigning priorities within a national VOC control programme, a number of indices may be used to focus on particular VOCs. The simplest but least effective approach is to focus on the relative mass emission, or relative ambient concentration.

11. Relative weighting based on OH reactivity addresses some but by no means all of the important aspects of the atmospheric reactions which generate ozone in the presence of NO_x and sunlight. The SAPRC (Statewide Air Pollution Research Center) weightings address

the situation in California. Because of differences in the model conditions appropriate to the Los Angeles basin and Europe, major differences in the fates of photochemical, labile species, such as aldehyde, result. POCPs calculated with photochemical models in the Netherlands, United States of America, United Kingdom, Sweden and by EMEP (MSC-W) address different aspects of the ozone problem in Europe.

12. Some of the less-reactive solvents cause other problems, e.g. they are extremely harmful to human health, difficult to handle, persistent, can cause negative environmental effects at other levels (e.g. in the free troposphere or the stratosphere). In many cases the best available technology for reducing solvent emission is the application of non-solvent using systems.

13. Reliable VOC emission inventories are essential to the formulation of any cost-effective VOC control policies and in particular those based on the POCP approach. National VOC emissions should therefore be specified according to sectors, at least following guidelines specified by the Executive Body, and should as far as possible be complemented by data on species and time variations of emissions.

TABLE 1

Classification of VOCs into three groups according to their importance in episodic ozone formation

More important

Alkenes	
Aromatics	
Alkanes	> C6 alkanes except 2,3 dimethylpentane
Aldehydes	All aldehydes except benzaldehyde
Biogenics	Isoprene

Less important

Alkanes	C3-C5 alkanes and 2,3 dimethylpentane
Ketones	Methyl ethyl ketone and methyl t-butyl ketone
Alcohols	Ethanol
Esters	All esters except methyl acetate

Least important

Alkanes	Methane and ethane
Alkynes	Acetylene
Aromatics	Benzene
Aldehydes	Benzaldehyde
Ketones	Acetone
Alcohols	Methanol
Esters	Methyl acetate
Chlorinated hydrocarbons	Methyl chloroform
	Methylene chloride
	Trichloroethylene and tetrachloroethylene

TABLE 2

Sectoral POCPs of the various emission sectors and the percentage by mass of VOCs in each ozone creation class

Sector	Sectoral POCP		Percentage mass in each ozone creation class			
	Canada	United Kingdom	More	Less Important	Least	Unknown
Petrol-engined vehicle exhaust	63	61	76	16	7	1
Diesel vehicle exhaust	60	59	38	19	3	39
Petrol-engined vehicle evaporation	–	51	57	29	2	12
Other transport	63	–	–	–	–	–
Stationary combustion	–	54	34	24	24	18
Solvent usage	42	40	49	26	21	3
Surface coating	48	51	–	–	–	–
Industrial process emissions	45	32	4	41	0	55
Industrial chemicals	70	63	–	–	–	–
Petroleum refining and distribution	54	45	55	42	1	2
Natural gas leakage	–	19	24	8	66	2
Agriculture	–	40	–	–	100	–
Coal mining	–	0	–	–	100	–
Domestic waste landfill	–	0	–	–	100	–
Dry cleaning	29	–	–	–	–	–
Wood combustion	55	–	–	–	–	–
Slash burn	58	–	–	–	–	–
Food industry	–	37	–	–	–	–

TABLE 3

Comparison between weighting schemes (expressed relative to ethylene = 100) for 85 VOC species

VOC	OH Scale [a]	Canada by mass [b]	SAPRC MIR [c]	UK POCP [d]	UK range [e]	Sweden max. diff. [f]	Sweden 0-4 days [g]	EMEP [h]	LOTOS [i]
Methane	0.1	–	0	0.7	0-3	–	–	–	–
Ethane	3.2	91.2	2.7	8.2	2-30	17.3	12.6	5-24	6-25
Propane	9.3	100	6.2	42.1	16-124	60.4	50.3	–	–
n-Butane	15.3	212	11.7	41.4	15-115	55.4	46.7	22-85	25-87
i-Butane	14.2	103	15.7	31.5	19-59	33.1	41.1	–	–
n-Pentane	19.4	109	12.1	40.8	9-105	61.2	29.8	–	–
i-Pentane	18.8	210	16.2	29.6	12-68	36.0	31.4	–	–
n-Hexane	22.5	71	11.5	42.1	10-151	78.4	45.2	–	–
2-Methylpentane	22.2	100	17.0	52.4	19-140	71.2	52.9	–	–
3-Methylpentane	22.6	47	17.7	43.1	11-125	64.7	40.9	–	–
2, 2-Dimethylbutane	10.5	–	7.5	25.1	12-49	–	–	–	–
2, 3-Dimethylbutane	25.0	–	13.8	38.4	25-65	–	–	–	–
n-Heptane	25.3	41	9.4	52.9	13-165	79.1	51.8	–	–
2-Methylhexane	18.4	21	17.0	49.2	11-159	–	–	–	–
3-Methylhexane	18.4	24	16.0	49.2	11-157	–	–	–	–
n-Octane	26.6	–	7.4	49.3	12-151	69.8	46.1	–	–
2-Methylheptane	26.6	–	16.0	46.9	12-146	69.1	45.7	–	–
n-Nonane	27.4	–	6.2	46.9	10-148	63.3	35.1	–	–
2-Methyloctane	27.3	–	13.2	50.5	12-147	66.9	45.4	–	–
n-Decane	27.6	–	5.3	46.4	8-156	71.9	42.2	–	–
2-Methylnonane	27.9	–	11.7	44.8	8-153	71.9	42.3	–	–
n-Undecane	29.6	21	4.7	43.6	8-144	66.2	38.6	–	–
n-Duodecane	28.4	–	4.3	41.2	7-138	57.6	31.1	–	–
Methylcyclohexane	35.7	18	22.3	–	–	40.3	38.6	–	–
Methylene chloride	–	–	–	1	0-3	0	0	–	–
Chloroform	–	–	–	–	–	0.7	0.4	–	–
Methyl chloroform	–	–	–	0.1	0-1	0.2	0.2	–	–
Trichloroethylene	–	–	–	6.6	1-13	8.6	11.1	–	–
Tetrachloroethylene	–	–	–	0.5	0-2	1.4	1.4	–	–
Allyl chloride	–	–	–	–	–	56.1	48.3	–	–
Methanol	10.9	–	7	12.3	9-21	16.5	21.3	–	–
Ethanol	25.5	–	15	26.8	4-89	44.6	22.5	9-58	20-71
i-Propanol	30.6	–	7	–	–	17.3	20.3	–	–
Butanol	38.9	–	30	–	–	65.5	21.4	–	–
i-Butanol	45.4	–	14	–	–	38.8	25.5	–	–
Ethylene glycol	41.4	–	21	–	–	–	–	–	–
Propylene glycol	55.2	–	18	–	–	–	–	–	–
But-2-diol	–	–	–	–	–	28.8	6.6	–	–

TABLE 3 (*continued*)

VOC	OH Scale [a]	Canada by mass [b]	SAPRC MIR [c]	UK POCP [d]	UK range [e]	Sweden max. diff. [f]	Sweden 0-4 days [g]	EMEP [h]	LOTOS [i]
Dimethyl ether	22.3	–	11	–	–	28.8	34.3	–	–
Methyl-t-butyl ether	11.1	–	8	–	–	–	–	–	–
Ethyl-t-butyl ether	25.2	–	26	–	–	–	–	–	–
Acetone	1.4	–	7	17.8	10-27	17.3	12.4	–	–
Methyl ethyl ketone	5.5	–	14	47.3	17-80	38.8	17.8	–	–
Methyl-i-butyl ketone	–	–	–	–	–	67.6	31.8	–	–
Methyl acetate	–	–	–	2.5	0-7	5.8	6.7	–	–
Ethyl acetate	–	–	–	21.8	11-56	29.5	29.4	–	–
i-Propyl acetate	–	–	–	21.5	14-36	–	–	–	–
n-Butyl acetate	–	–	–	32.3	14-91	43.9	32.0	–	–
i-Butyl acetate	–	–	–	33.2	21-59	28.8	35.3	–	–
Propylene glycol methyl ether	–	–	–	–	–	77.0	49.1	–	–
Propylene glycol methyl ether acetate	–	–	–	–	–	30.9	15.7	–	–
Ethylene	100	100	100	100	100	100	100	100	100
Propylene	217	44	125	103	75-163	73.4	59.9	69-138	55-120
1-Butene	194	32	115	95.9	57-185	79.9	49.5	–	–
2-Butene	371	–	136	99.2	82-157	78.4	43.6	–	–
1-Pentene	148	–	79	105.9	40-288	72.7	42.4	–	–
2-Pentene	327	–	79	93.0	65-160	77.0	38.1	–	–
2-Methyl-1-butene	300	–	70	77.7	52-113	69.1	18.1	–	–
2-Methyl-2-butene	431	24	93	77.9	61-102	93.5	45.3	–	–
3-Methyl-1-butene	158	–	79	89.5	60-154	–	–	–	–
Isobutene	318	50	77	64.3	58-76	79.1	58.0	–	–
Isoprene	515	–	121	–	–	53.2	58.3	–	–
Acetylene	10.4	82	6.8	16.8	10-42	27.3	36.8	–	–
Benzene	5.7	71	5.3	18.9	11-45	31.7	40.2	–	–
Toluene	23.4	218	34	56.3	41-83	44.6	47.0	–	–
o-Xylene	48.3	38	87	66.6	41-97	42.4	16.7	54-112	26-67
m-Xylene	80.2	53	109	99.3	78-135	58.3	47.4	–	–
p-Xylene	49.7	53	89	88.8	63-180	61.2	47.2	–	–
Ethylbenzene	25	32	36	59.3	35-114	53.2	50.4	–	–
1, 2, 3-Trimethyl benzene	89	–	119	117	76-175	69.8	29.2	–	–
1, 2, 4-Trimethyl benzene	107	44	119	120	86-176	68.3	33.0	–	–
1, 3, 5-Trimethyl benzene	159	–	140	115	74-174	69.1	33.0	–	–
o-Ethyltoluene	35.	–	96	66.8	31-130	59.7	40.8	–	–
m-Ethyltoluene	50	–	96	79.4	41-140	62.6	40.1	–	–
p-Ethyltoluene	33	–	96	72.5	36-135	62.6	44.3	–	–
n-Propylbenzene	17	–	28	49.2	25-110	51.1	45.4	–	–
i-Propylbenzene	18	–	30	56.5	35-105	51.1	52.3	–	–
Formaldehyde	104	–	117	42.1	22-58	42.4	26.1	–	–
Acetaldehyde	128	–	72	52.7	33-122	53.2	18.6	–	–
Proprionaldehyde	117	–	87	60.3	28-160	65.5	17.0	–	–
Butyraldehyde	124	–	–	56.8	16-160	64.0	17.1	–	–
i-Butyraldehyde	144	–	–	63.1	38-128	58.3	30.0	–	–
Valeraldehyde	112	–	–	68.6	0-268	61.2	32.1	–	–
Acrolein	–	–	–	–	–	120.1	82.3	–	–
Benzaldehyde	43	–	10	33.4	−82-(−12)	–	–	–	–

[a] OH + VOC rate coefficient divided by molecular weight.

[b] Ambient VOC concentrations at 18 sites in Canada expressed on mass basics.

[c] Maximum Incremental Reactivity (MIR) based on California scenarios; Statewide Air Pollution Research Center, Los Angeles, USA.

[d] Average POCP based on three scenarios and 9 days; FRG-Ireland, France-Sweden and UK.

[e] Range of POCPs based on three scenarios and 11 days.

[f] POCPs calculated for a single source in Sweden producing maximum ozone difference.

[g] POCPs calculated for a single source in Sweden using average difference in ozone over 4 days.

[h] Range (5th-95th percentile) of POCPs calculated over EMEP grid.

[i] Range (20th-80th percentile) of POCPs calculated over LOTOS grid.

$$POCP = \frac{\frac{a}{b}}{\frac{c}{d}} \times 100$$

where
(a) — Change in photochemical oxidant formation due to a change in a VOC emission
(b) — Integrated VOC emission up to that time
(c) — Change in photochemical oxidant formation due to a change in ethylene emissions
(d) — Integrated ethylene emission up to that time

It is a quantity derived from a photochemical ozone model by following the photochemical ozone production with and without the presence of an individual hydrocarbon. The difference in ozone concentrations between such pairs of model calculations is a measure of the contribution that VOC makes in ozone formation.

CONVENTION ON ENVIRONMENTAL IMPACT ASSESSMENT IN A TRANSBOUNDARY CONTEXT

CONVENTION ON ENVIRONMENTAL IMPACT ASSESSMENT IN A TRANSBOUNDARY CONTEXT

The Parties to this Convention,

Aware of the interrelationship between economic activities and their environmental consequences,

Affirming the need to ensure environmentally sound and sustainable development,

Determined to enhance international cooperation in assessing environmental impact in particular in a transboundary context,

Mindful of the need and importance to develop anticipatory policies and of preventing, mitigating and monitoring significant adverse environmental impact in general and more specifically in a transboundary context,

Recalling the relevant provisions of the Charter of the United Nations, the Declaration of the Stockholm Conference on the Human Environment, the Final Act of the Conference on Security and Cooperation in Europe (CSCE) and the Concluding Documents of the Madrid and Vienna Meetings of Representatives of the Participating States of the CSCE,

Commending the ongoing activities of States to ensure that, through their national legal and administrative provisions and their national policies, environmental impact assessment is carried out,

Conscious of the need to give explicit consideration to environmental factors at an early stage in the decision-making process by applying environmental impact assessment, at all appropriate administrative levels, as a necessary tool to improve the quality of information presented to decision makers so that environmentally sound decisions can be made paying careful attention to minimizing significant adverse impact, particularly in a transboundary context,

Mindful of the efforts of international organizations to promote the use of environmental impact assessment both at the national and international levels, and taking into account work on environmental impact assessment carried out under the auspices of the United Nations Economic Commission for Europe, in particular results achieved by the Seminar on Environmental Impact Assessment (September 1987, Warsaw, Poland) as well as noting the Goals and Principles on environmental impact assessment adopted by the Governing Council of the United Nations Environment Programme, and the Ministerial Declaration on Sustainable Development (May 1990, Bergen, Norway),

Have agreed as follows:

Article 1

DEFINITIONS

For the purposes of this Convention,

(i) "Parties" means, unless the text otherwise indicates, the Contracting Parties to this Convention;

(ii) "Party of origin" means the Contracting Party or Parties to this Convention under whose jurisdiction a proposed activity is envisaged to take place;

(iii) "Affected Party" means the Contracting Party or Parties to this Convention likely to be affected by the transboundary impact of a proposed activity;

(iv) "Concerned Parties" means the Party of origin and the affected Party of an environmental impact assessment pursuant to this Convention;

(v) "Proposed activity" means any activity or any major change to an activity subject to a decision of a competent authority in accordance with an applicable national procedure;

(vi) "Environmental impact assessment" means a national procedure for evaluating the likely impact of a proposed activity on the environment;

(vii) "Impact" means any effect caused by a proposed activity on the environment including human health and safety, flora, fauna, soil, air, water, climate, landscape and historical monuments or other physical structures or the interaction among these factors; it also includes effects on cultural heritage or socio-economic conditions resulting from alterations to those factors;

(viii) "Transboundary impact" means any impact, not exclusively of a global nature, within an area under the jurisdiction of a Party caused by a proposed activity the physical origin of which is situated wholly or in part within the area under the jurisdiction of another Party;

(ix) "Competent authority" means the national authority or authorities designated by a Party as responsible for performing the tasks covered by this Convention and/or the authority or authorities entrusted by a Party with decision-making powers regarding a proposed activity;

(x) "The Public" means one or more natural or legal persons.

Article 2

GENERAL PROVISIONS

1. The Parties shall, either individually or jointly, take all appropriate and effective measures to prevent, reduce and control significant adverse transboundary environmental impact from proposed activities.

2. Each Party shall take the necessary legal, administrative or other measures to implement the provisions of this Convention, including, with respect to proposed activities listed in Appendix I that are likely to cause significant adverse transboundary impact, the establishment of an environmental impact assessment procedure that permits public participation and preparation of the environmental impact assessment documentation described in Appendix II.

3. The Party of origin shall ensure that in accordance with the provisions of this Convention an environmental impact assessment is undertaken prior to a decision to authorize or undertake a proposed activity listed in Appendix I that is likely to cause a significant adverse transboundary impact.

4. The Party of origin shall, consistent with the provisions of this Convention, ensure that affected Parties are notified of a proposed activity listed in Appendix I that is likely to cause a significant adverse transboundary impact.

5. Concerned Parties shall, at the initiative of any such Party, enter into discussions on whether one or more proposed activities not listed in Appendix I is or are likely to cause a significant adverse transboundary impact and thus should be treated as if it or they were so listed. Where those Parties so agree, the activity or activities shall be thus treated. General guidance for identifying criteria to determine significant adverse impact is set forth in Appendix III.

6. The Party of origin shall provide, in accordance with the provisions of this Convention, an opportunity to the public in the areas likely to be affected to participate in relevant environmental impact assessment procedures regarding proposed activities and shall ensure that the opportunity provided to the public of the affected Party is equivalent to that provided to the public of the Party of origin.

7. Environmental impact assessments as required by this Convention shall, as a minimum requirement, be undertaken at the project level of the proposed activity. To the extent appropriate, the Parties shall endeavour to apply the principles of environmental impact assessment to policies, plans and programmes.

8. The provisions of this Convention shall not affect the right of Parties to implement national laws, regulations, administrative provisions or accepted legal practices protecting information the supply of which would be prejudicial to industrial and commercial secrecy or national security.

9. The provisions of this Convention shall not affect the right of particular Parties to implement, by bilateral or multilateral agreement where appropriate, more stringent measures than those of this Convention.

10. The provisions of this Convention shall not prejudice any obligations of the Parties under international law with regard to activities having or likely to have a transboundary impact.

Article 3

NOTIFICATION

1. For a proposed activity listed in Appendix I that is likely to cause a significant adverse transboundary impact, the Party of origin shall, for the purposes of ensuring adequate and effective consultations under Article 5, notify any Party which it considers may be an affected Party as early as possible and no later than when informing its own public about that proposed activity.

2. This notification shall contain, *inter alia*:

(*a*) Information on the proposed activity, including any available information on its possible transboundary impact;

(*b*) The nature of the possible decision; and

(*c*) An indication of a reasonable time within which a response under paragraph 3 of this Article is required, taking into account the nature of the proposed activity;

and may include the information set out in paragraph 5 of this Article.

3. The affected Party shall respond to the Party of origin within the time specified in the notification, acknowledging receipt of the notification, and shall indicate whether it intends to participate in the environmental impact assessment procedure.

4. If the affected Party indicates that it does not intend to participate in the environmental impact assessment procedure, or if it does not respond within the time specified in the notification, the provisions in paragraphs 5, 6, 7 and 8 of this Article and in Articles 4 to 7 will not apply. In such circumstances the right of a Party of origin to determine whether to carry out an environmental impact assessment on the basis of its national law and practice is not prejudiced.

5. Upon receipt of a response from the affected Party indicating its desire to participate in the environmental impact assessment procedure, the Party of origin shall, if it has not already done so, provide to the affected Party:

(*a*) Relevant information regarding the environmental impact assessment procedure, including an indication of the time schedule for transmittal of comments; and (*b*) Relevant information on the proposed activity and its possible significant adverse transboundary impact.

6. An affected Party shall, at the request of the Party of origin, provide the latter with reasonably obtainable information relating to the potentially affected environment under the jurisdiction of the affected Party, where such information is necessary for the preparation of the environmental impact assessment documentation. The information shall be furnished promptly and, as appropriate, through a joint body where one exists.

7. When a Party considers that it would be affected by a significant adverse transboundary impact of a proposed activity listed in Appendix I, and when no notification has taken place in accordance with paragraph 1 of this Article, the concerned Parties shall, at the request of the affected Party, exchange sufficient information for the purposes of holding discussions on whether there is likely to be a significant adverse transboundary impact. If those Parties agree that there is likely to be a significant adverse transboundary impact, the provisions of this Convention shall apply accordingly. If those Parties cannot agree whether there is likely to be a significant adverse transboundary impact, any such Party may submit that question to an inquiry commission in accordance with the provisions of Appendix IV to advise on the likelihood of significant adverse transboundary impact, unless they agree on another method of settling this question.

8. The concerned Parties shall ensure that the public of the affected Party in the areas likely to be affected be informed of, and be provided with possibilities for making comments or objections on, the proposed activity, and for the transmittal of these comments or objections to the competent authority of the Party of origin, either directly to this authority or, where appropriate, through the Party of origin.

Article 4

PREPARATION OF THE ENVIRONMENTAL IMPACT ASSESSMENT DOCUMENTATION

1. The environmental impact assessment documentation to be submitted to the competent authority of the Party of origin shall contain, as a minimum, the information described in Appendix II.

2. The Party of origin shall furnish the affected Party, as appropriate through a joint body where one exists, with the environmental impact assessment documentation. The concerned Parties shall arrange for distribution of the documentation to the authorities and the public of the affected Party in the areas likely to be affected and for the submission of comments to the competent authority of the Party of origin, either directly to this authority or, where appropriate, through the Party of origin within a reasonable time before the final decision is taken on the proposed activity.

Article 5

CONSULTATIONS ON THE BASIS OF THE ENVIRONMENTAL IMPACT ASSESSMENT DOCUMENTATION

The Party of origin shall, after completion of the environmental impact assessment documentation, without undue delay enter into consultations with the affected Party concerning, *inter alia*, the potential transboundary impact of the proposed activity and measures to reduce or eliminate its impact. Consultations may relate to:

(*a*) Possible alternatives to the proposed activity, including the no-action alternative and possible measures to mitigate significant adverse transboundary impact and to monitor the effects of such measures at the expense of the Party of origin;

(*b*) Other forms of possible mutual assistance in reducing any significant adverse transboundary impact of the proposed activity; and

(*c*) Any other appropriate matters relating to the proposed activity.

The Parties shall agree, at the commencement of such consultations, on a reasonable time-frame for the duration of the consultation period. Any such consultations may be conducted through an appropriate joint body, where one exists.

Article 6

FINAL DECISION

1. The Parties shall ensure that, in the final decision on the proposed activity, due account is taken of the outcome of the environmental impact assessment, including the environmental impact assessment documentation, as well as the comments thereon received pursuant to Article 3, paragraph 8 and Article 4, paragraph 2, and the outcome of the consultations as referred to in Article 5.

2. The Party of origin shall provide to the affected Party the final decision on the proposed activity along with the reasons and considerations on which it was based.

3. If additional information on the significant transboundary impact of a proposed activity, which was not available at the time a decision was made with respect to that activity and which could have materially affected the decision, becomes available to a concerned Party before work on that activity commences, that Party shall immediately inform the other concerned Party or Parties. If one of the concerned Parties so requests, consultations shall be held as to whether the decision needs to be revised.

Article 7

POST-PROJECT ANALYSIS

1. The concerned Parties, at the request of any such Party, shall determine whether, and if so to what extent, a post-project analysis shall be carried out, taking into account the likely significant adverse transboundary impact of the activity for which an environmental impact assessment has been undertaken pursuant to this Convention. Any post-project analysis undertaken shall include, in particular, the surveillance of the activity and the determination of any adverse transboundary impact. Such surveillance and determination may be undertaken with a view to achieving the objectives listed in Appendix V.

2. When, as a result of post-project analysis, the Party of origin or the affected Party has reasonable grounds for concluding that there is a significant adverse transboundary impact or factors have been discovered which may result in such an impact, it shall immediately inform the other Party. The concerned Parties shall then consult on necessary measures to reduce or eliminate the impact.

Article 8

BILATERAL AND MULTILATERAL COOPERATION

The Parties may continue existing or enter into new bilateral or multilateral agreements or other arrangements in order to implement their obligations under this Convention. Such agreements or other arrangements may be based on the elements listed in Appendix VI.

Article 9

RESEARCH PROGRAMMES

The Parties shall give special consideration to the setting up, or intensification of, specific research programmes aimed at:

(*a*) Improving existing qualitative and quantitative methods for assessing the impacts of proposed activities;

(*b*) Achieving a better understanding of cause-effect relationships and their role in integrated environmental management;

(*c*) Analysing and monitoring the efficient implementation of decisions on proposed activities with the intention of minimizing or preventing impacts;

(*d*) Developing methods to stimulate creative approaches in the search for environmentally sound alternatives to proposed activities, production and consumption patterns;

(*e*) Developing methodologies for the application of the principles of environmental impact assessment at the macroeconomic level.

The results of the programmes listed above shall be exchanged by the Parties.

Article 10

STATUS OF THE APPENDICES

The Appendices attached to this Convention form an integral part of the Convention.

Article 11

MEETING OF PARTIES

1. The Parties shall meet, so far as possible, in connection with the annual sessions of the Senior Advisers to ECE Governments on Environmental and Water Problems. The first meeting of the Parties shall be convened not later than one year after the date of the entry into force of this Convention. Thereafter, meetings of the Parties shall be held at such other times as may be deemed necessary by a meeting of the Parties, or at the written request of any Party, provided that, within six months of the request being communicated to them by the secretariat, it is supported by at least one third of the Parties.

2. The Parties shall keep under continuous review the implementation of this Convention, and, with this purpose in mind, shall:

(*a*) Review the policies and methodological approaches to environmental impact assessment by the Parties with a view to further improving environmental impact assessment procedures in a transboundary context;

(*b*) Exchange information regarding experience gained in concluding and implementing bilateral and multilateral agreements or other arrangements regarding the use of environmental impact assessment in a transboundary context to which one or more of the Parties are party;

(*c*) Seek, where appropriate, the services of competent international bodies and scientific committees in methodological and technical aspects pertinent to the achievement of the purposes of this Convention;

(*d*) At their first meeting, consider and by consensus adopt rules of procedure for their meetings;

(*e*) Consider and, where necessary, adopt proposals for amendments to this Convention;

(*f*) Consider and undertake any additional action that may be required for the achievement of the purposes of this Convention.

Article 12

RIGHT TO VOTE

1. Each Party to this Convention shall have one vote.

2. Except as provided for in paragraph 1 of this Article, regional economic integration organizations, in matters within their competence, shall exercise their right to vote with a number of votes equal to the number of their member States which are Parties to this Convention. Such organizations shall not exercise their right to vote if their member States exercise theirs, and vice versa.

Article 13

SECRETARIAT

The Executive Secretary of the Economic Commission for Europe shall carry out the following secretariat functions:

(a) The convening and preparing of meetings of the Parties;

(b) The transmission of reports and other information received in accordance with the provisions of this Convention to the Parties; and

(c) The performance of other functions as may be provided for in this Convention or as may be determined by the Parties.

Article 14

AMENDMENTS TO THE CONVENTION

1. Any Party may propose amendments to this Convention.

2. Proposed amendments shall be submitted in writing to the secretariat, which shall communicate them to all Parties. The proposed amendments shall be discussed at the next meeting of the Parties, provided these proposals have been circulated by the secretariat to the Parties at least ninety days in advance.

3. The Parties shall make every effort to reach agreement on any proposed amendment to this Convention by consensus. If all efforts at consensus have been exhausted, and no agreement reached, the amendment shall as a last resort be adopted by a three-fourths majority vote of the Parties present and voting at the meeting.

4. Amendments to this Convention adopted in accordance with paragraph 3 of this Article shall be submitted by the Depositary to all Parties for ratification, approval or acceptance. They shall enter into force for Parties having ratified, approved or accepted them on the ninetieth day after the receipt by the Depositary of notification of their ratification, approval or acceptance by at least three-fourths of these Parties. Thereafter they shall enter into force for any other Party on the ninetieth day after that Party deposits its instrument of ratification, approval or acceptance of the amendments.

5. For the purpose of this Article, "Parties present and voting" means Parties present and casting an affirmative or negative vote.

6. The voting procedure set forth in paragraph 3 of this Article is not intended to constitute a precedent for future agreements negotiated within the Economic Commission for Europe.

Article 15

SETTLEMENT OF DISPUTES

1. If a dispute arises between two or more Parties about the interpretation or application of this Convention, they shall seek a solution by negotiation or by any other method of dispute settlement acceptable to the parties to the dispute.

2. When signing, ratifying, accepting, approving or acceding to this Convention, or at any time thereafter, a Party may declare in writing to the Depositary that for a dispute not resolved in accordance with paragraph 1 of this Article, it accepts one or both of the following means of dispute settlement as compulsory in relation to any Party accepting the same obligation:

(a) Submission of the dispute to the International Court of Justice;

(b) Arbitration in accordance with the procedure set out in Appendix VII.

3. If the parties to the dispute have accepted both means of dispute settlement referred to in paragraph 2 of this Article, the dispute may be submitted only to the International Court of Justice, unless the parties agree otherwise.

Article 16

SIGNATURE

This Convention shall be open for signature at Espoo (Finland) from 25 February to 1 March 1991 and thereafter at United Nations Headquarters in New York until 2 September 1991 by States members of the Economic Commission for Europe as well as States having consultative status with the Economic Commission for Europe pursuant to paragraph 8 of the Economic and Social Council resolution 36 (IV) of 28 March 1947, and by regional economic integration organizations constituted by sovereign States members of the Economic Commission for Europe to which their member States have transferred competence in respect of matters governed by this Convention, including the competence to enter into treaties in respect of these matters.

Article 17

RATIFICATION, ACCEPTANCE, APPROVAL AND ACCESSION

1. This Convention shall be subject to ratification, acceptance or approval by signatory States and regional economic integration organizations.

2. This Convention shall be open for accession as from 3 September 1991 by the States and organizations referred to in Article 16.

3. The instruments of ratification, acceptance, approval or accession shall be deposited with the Secretary-General of the United Nations, who shall perform the functions of Depositary.

4. Any organization referred to in Article 16 which becomes a Party to this Convention without any of its member States being a Party shall be bound by all the obligations under this Convention. In the case of such organizations, one or more of whose member States is a Party to this Convention, the organization and its member States shall decide on their respective responsibilities for the performance of their obligations under this Convention. In such cases, the organization and the member States shall not be entitled to exercise rights under this Convention concurrently.

5. In their instruments of ratification, acceptance, approval or accession, the regional economic integration organizations referred to in Article 16 shall declare the extent of their competence with respect to the matters governed by this Convention. These organizations shall also inform the Depositary of any relevant modification to the extent of their competence.

Article 18

ENTRY INTO FORCE

1. This Convention shall enter into force on the ninetieth day after the date of deposit of the sixteenth instrument of ratification, acceptance, approval or accession.

2. For the purposes of paragraph 1 of this Article, any instrument deposited by a regional economic integration organization shall not be counted as additional to those deposited by States members of such an organization.

3. For each State or organization referred to in Article 16 which ratifies, accepts or approves this Convention or accedes thereto after the deposit of the sixteenth instrument of ratification, acceptance, approval or accession, this Convention shall enter into force on the ninetieth day after the date of deposit by such State or organization of its instrument of ratification, acceptance, approval or accession.

Article 19

WITHDRAWAL

At any time after four years from the date on which this Convention has come into force with respect to a Party, that Party may withdraw from this Convention by giving written notification to the Depositary. Any such withdrawal shall take effect on the ninetieth day after the date of its receipt by the Depositary. Any such withdrawal shall not affect the application of Articles 3 to 6 of this Convention to a proposed activity in respect of which a notification has been made pursuant to Article 3, paragraph 1, or a request has been made pursuant to Article 3, paragraph 7, before such withdrawal took effect.

Article 20

AUTHENTIC TEXTS

The original of this Convention, of which the English, French and Russian texts are equally authentic, shall be deposited with the Secretary-General of the United Nations.

IN WITNESS WHEREOF the undersigned, being duly authorized thereto, have signed this Convention.

DONE at Espoo (Finland), this twenty-fifth day of February one thousand nine hundred and ninety-one.

APPENDICES

APPENDIX I

List of activities

1. Crude oil refineries (excluding undertakings manufacturing only lubricants from crude oil) and installations for the gasification and liquefaction of 500 tonnes or more of coal or bituminous shale per day.

2. Thermal power stations and other combustion installations with a heat output of 300 megawatts or more and nuclear power stations and other nuclear reactors (except research installations for the production and conversion of fissionable and fertile materials, whose maximum power does not exceed 1 kilowatt continuous thermal load).

3. Installations solely designed for the production or enrichment of nuclear fuels, for the reprocessing of irradiated nuclear fuels or for the storage, disposal and processing of radioactive waste.

4. Major installations for the initial smelting of cast-iron and steel and for the production of non-ferrous metals.

5. Installations for the extraction of asbestos and for the processing and transformation of asbestos and products containing asbestos: for asbestos-cement products, with an annual production of more than 20,000 tonnes finished product; for friction material, with an annual production of more than 50 tonnes finished product; and for other asbestos utilization of more than 200 tonnes per year.

6. Integrated chemical installations.

7. Construction of motorways, express roads* and lines for long-distance railway traffic and of airports with a basic runway length of 2,100 metres or more.

8. Large-diameter oil and gas pipelines.

9. Trading ports and also inland waterways and ports for inland-waterway traffic which permit the passage of vessels of over 1,350 tonnes.

10. Waste-disposal installations for the incineration, chemical treatment or landfill of toxic and dangerous wastes.

11. Large dams and reservoirs.

12. Groundwater abstraction activities in cases where the annual volume of water to be abstracted amounts to 10 million cubic metres or more.

13. Pulp and paper manufacturing of 200 air-dried metric tonnes or more per day.

14. Major mining, on-site extraction and processing of metal ores or coal.

15. Offshore hydrocarbon production.

16. Major storage facilities for petroleum, petrochemical and chemical products.

17. Deforestation of large areas.

---

* For the purposes of this Convention:

"Motorway" means a road specially designed and built for motor traffic, which does not serve properties bordering on it, and which:

(a) Is provided, except at special points or temporarily, with separate carriageways for the two directions of traffic, separated from each other by a dividing strip not intended for traffic or, exceptionally, by other means;

(b) Does not cross at level with any road, railway or tramway track, or footpath; and

(c) Is specially sign-posted as a motorway.

"Express road" means a road reserved for motor traffic accessible only from interchanges or controlled junctions and on which, in particular, stopping and parking are prohibited on the running carriageway(s).

APPENDIX II

Content of the environmental impact assessment documentation

Information to be included in the environmental impact assessment documentation shall, as a minimum, contain, in accordance with Article 4:

(*a*) A description of the proposed activity and its purpose;

(*b*) A description, where appropriate, of reasonable alternatives (for example, locational or technological) to the proposed activity and also the no-action alternative;

(*c*) A description of the environment likely to be significantly affected by the proposed activity and its alternatives;

(*d*) A description of the potential environmental impact of the proposed activity and its alternatives and an estimation of its significance;

(*e*) A description of mitigation measures to keep adverse environmental impact to a minimum;

(*f*) An explicit indication of predictive methods and underlying assumptions as well as the relevant environmental data used;

(*g*) An identification of gaps in knowledge and uncertainties encountered in compiling the required information;

(*h*) Where appropriate, an outline for monitoring and management programmes and any plans for post-project analysis; and

(*i*) A non-technical summary including a visual presentation as appropriate (maps, graphs, etc.).

APPENDIX III

General criteria to assist in the determination of the environmental significance of activities not listed in Appendix I

1. In considering proposed activities to which Article 2, paragraph 5, applies, the concerned Parties may consider whether the activity is likely to have a significant adverse transboundary impact in particular by virtue of one or more of the following criteria:

(*a*) *Size*: proposed activities which are large for the type of the activity;

(*b*) *Location*: proposed activities which are located in or close to an area of special environmental sensitivity or importance (such as wetlands designated under the Ramsar Convention, national parks, nature reserves, sites of special scientific interest, or sites of archaeological, cultural or historical importance); also, proposed activities in locations where the characteristics of proposed devel-

opment would be likely to have significant effects on the population;

(*c*) *Effects*: proposed activities with particularly complex and potentially adverse effects, including those giving rise to serious effects on humans or on valued species or organisms, those which threaten the existing or potential use of an affected area and those causing additional loading which cannot be sustained by the carrying capacity of the environment.

2. The concerned Parties shall consider for this purpose proposed activities which are located close to an international frontier as well as more remote proposed activities which could give rise to significant transboundary effects far removed from the site of development.

APPENDIX IV

Inquiry procedure

1. The requesting Party or Parties shall notify the secretariat that it or they submit(s) the question of whether a proposed activity listed in Appendix I is likely to have a significant adverse transboundary impact to an inquiry commission established in accordance with the provisions of this Appendix. This notification shall state the subject-matter of the inquiry. The secretariat shall notify immediately all Parties to this Convention of this submission.

2. The inquiry commission shall consist of three members. Both the requesting party and the other party to the inquiry procedure shall appoint a scientific or technical expert, and the two experts so appointed shall designate by common agreement the third expert, who shall be the president of the inquiry commission. The latter shall not be a national of one of the parties to the inquiry procedure, nor have his or her usual place of residence in the territory of one of these parties, nor be employed by any of them, nor have dealt with the matter in any other capacity.

3. If the president of the inquiry commission has not been designated within two months of the appointment of the second expert, the Executive Secretary of the Economic Commission for Europe shall, at the request of either party, designate the president within a further two-month period.

4. If one of the parties to the inquiry procedure does not appoint an expert within one month of its receipt of the notification by the secretariat, the other party may inform the Executive Secretary of the Economic Commission for Europe, who shall designate the president of the inquiry commission within a further two-month period. Upon designation, the president of the inquiry commission shall request the party which has not appointed an expert to do so within one month. After such a period, the president shall inform the Executive Secretary of the Economic Commission for Europe, who shall make this appointment within a further two-month period.

5. The inquiry commission shall adopt its own rules of procedure.

6. The inquiry commission may take all appropriate measures in order to carry out its functions.

7. The parties to the inquiry procedure shall facilitate the work of the inquiry commission and, in particular, using all means at their disposal, shall:

(a) Provide it with all relevant documents, facilities and information; and

(b) Enable it, where necessary, to call witnesses or experts and receive their evidence.

8. The parties and the experts shall protect the confidentiality of any information they receive in confidence during the work of the inquiry commission.

9. If one of the parties to the inquiry procedure does not appear before the inquiry commission or fails to present its case, the other party may request the inquiry commission to continue the proceedings and to complete its work. Absence of a party or failure of a party to present its case shall not constitute a bar to the continuation and completion of the work of the inquiry commission.

10. Unless the inquiry commission determines otherwise because of the particular circumstances of the matter, the expenses of the inquiry commission, including the remuneration of its members, shall be borne by the parties to the inquiry procedure in equal shares. The inquiry commission shall keep a record of all its expenses, and shall furnish a final statement thereof to the parties.

11. Any Party having an interest of a factual nature in the subject-matter of the inquiry procedure, and which may be affected by an opinion in the matter, may intervene in the proceedings with the consent of the inquiry commission.

12. The decisions of the inquiry commission on matters of procedure shall be taken by majority vote of its members. The final opinion of the inquiry commission shall reflect the view of the majority of its members and shall include any dissenting view.

13. The inquiry commission shall present its final opinion within two months of the date on which it was established unless it finds it necessary to extend this time limit for a period which should not exceed two months.

14. The final opinion of the inquiry commission shall be based on accepted scientific principles. The final opinion shall be transmitted by the inquiry commission to the parties to the inquiry procedure and to the secretariat.

APPENDIX V

Post-project analysis

Objectives include:

(*a*) Monitoring compliance with the conditions as set out in the authorization or approval of the activity and the effectiveness of mitigation measures;

(*b*) Review of an impact for proper management and in order to cope with uncertainties;

(*c*) Verification of past predictions in order to transfer experience to future activities of the same type.

APPENDIX VI

Elements for bilateral and multilateral cooperation

1. Concerned Parties may set up, where appropriate, institutional arrangements or enlarge the mandate of existing institutional arrangements within the framework of bilateral and multilateral agreements in order to give full effect to this Convention.

2. Bilateral and multilateral agreements or other arrangements may include:

(*a*) Any additional requirements for the implementation of this Convention, taking into account the specific conditions of the subregion concerned;

(*b*) Institutional, administrative and other arrangements, to be made on a reciprocal and equivalent basis;

(*c*) Harmonization of their policies and measures for the protection of the environment in order to attain the greatest possible similarity in standards and methods related to the implementation of environmental impact assessment;

(*d*) Developing, improving, and/or harmonizing methods for the identification, measurement, prediction and assessment of impacts, and for post-project analysis;

(*e*) Developing and/or improving methods and programmes for the collection, analysis, storage and timely dissemination of comparable data regarding environmental quality in order to provide input into environmental impact assessment;

(*f*) The establishment of threshold levels and more specified criteria for defining the significance of transboundary impacts related to the location, nature or size of proposed activities, for which environmental impact assessment in accordance with the provisions of this Convention shall be applied; and the establishment of critical loads of transboundary pollution;

(*g*) Undertaking, where appropriate, joint environmental impact assessment, development of joint monitoring programmes, intercalibration of monitoring devices and harmonization of methodologies with a view to rendering the data and information obtained compatible.

APPENDIX VII

Arbitration

1. The claimant Party or Parties shall notify the secretariat that the Parties have agreed to submit the dispute to arbitration pursuant to Article 15, paragraph 2, of this Convention. The notification shall state the subject-matter of arbitration and include, in particular, the Articles of this Convention, the interpretation or application of which are at issue. The secretariat shall forward the information received to all Parties to this Convention.

2. The arbitral tribunal shall consist of three members. Both the claimant Party or Parties and the other Party or Parties to the dispute shall appoint an arbitrator, and the two arbitrators so appointed shall designate by common agreement the third arbitrator, who shall be the president of the arbitral tribunal. The latter shall not be a national of one of the parties to the dispute, nor have his or her usual place of residence in the territory of one of

these parties, nor be employed by any of them, nor have dealt with the case in any other capacity.

3. If the president of the arbitral tribunal has not been designated within two months of the appointment of the second arbitrator, the Executive Secretary of the Economic Commission for Europe shall, at the request of either party to the dispute, designate the president within a further two-month period.

4. If one of the parties to the dispute does not appoint an arbitrator within two months of the receipt of the request, the other party may inform the Executive Secretary of the Economic Commission for Europe, who shall designate the president of the arbitral tribunal within a further two-month period. Upon designation, the president of the arbitral tribunal shall request the party which has not appointed an arbitrator to do so within two months. After such a period, the president shall inform the Executive Secretary of the Economic Commission for Europe, who shall make this appointment within a further two-month period.

5. The arbitral tribunal shall render its decision in accordance with international law and in accordance with the provisions of this Convention.

6. Any arbitral tribunal constituted under the provisions set out herein shall draw up its own rules of procedure.

7. The decisions of the arbitral tribunal, both on procedure and on substance, shall be taken by majority vote of its members.

8. The tribunal may take all appropriate measures in order to establish the facts.

9. The parties to the dispute shall facilitate the work of the arbitral tribunal and, in particular, using all means at their disposal, shall:

(*a*) Provide it with all relevant documents, facilities and information; and

(*b*) Enable it, where necessary, to call witnesses or experts and receive their evidence.

10. The parties and the arbitrators shall protect the confidentiality of any information they receive in confidence during the proceedings of the arbitral tribunal.

11. The arbitral tribunal may, at the request of one of the parties, recommend interim measures of protection.

12. If one of the parties to the dispute does not appear before the arbitral tribunal or fails to defend its case, the other party may request the tribunal to continue the proceedings and to render its final decision. Absence of a party or failure of a party to defend its case shall not constitute a bar to the proceedings. Before rendering its final decision, the arbitral tribunal must satisfy itself that the claim is well founded in fact and law.

13. The arbitral tribunal may hear and determine counter-claims arising directly out of the subject-matter of the dispute.

14. Unless the arbitral tribunal determines otherwise because of the particular circumstances of the case, the expenses of the tribunal, including the remuneration of its members, shall be borne by the parties to the dispute in equal shares. The tribunal shall keep a record of all its expenses, and shall furnish a final statement thereof to the parties.

15. Any Party to this Convention having an interest of a legal nature in the subject-matter of the dispute, and which may be affected by a decision in the case, may intervene in the proceedings with the consent of the tribunal.

16. The arbitral tribunal shall render its award within five months of the date on which it is established unless it finds it necessary to extend the time limit for a period which should not exceed five months.

17. The award of the arbitral tribunal shall be accompanied by a statement of reasons. It shall be final and binding upon all parties to the dispute. The award will be transmitted by the arbitral tribunal to the parties to the dispute and to the secretariat. The secretariat will forward the information received to all Parties to this Convention.

18. Any dispute which may arise between the parties concerning the interpretation or execution of the award may be submitted by either party to the arbitral tribunal which made the award or, if the latter cannot be seized thereof, to another tribunal constituted for this purpose in the same manner as the first.

CONVENTION ON THE TRANSBOUNDARY EFFECTS OF INDUSTRIAL ACCIDENTS

CONVENTION ON THE TRANSBOUNDARY EFFECTS
OF INDUSTRIAL ACCIDENTS

PREAMBLE

The Parties to this Convention,

Mindful of the special importance, in the interest of present and future generations, of protecting human beings and the environment against the effects of industrial accidents,

Recognizing the importance and urgency of preventing serious adverse effects of industrial accidents on human beings and the environment, and of promoting all measures that stimulate the rational, economic and efficient use of preventive, preparedness and response measures to enable environmentally sound and sustainable economic development,

Taking into account the fact that the effects of industrial accidents may make themselves felt across borders, and require cooperation among States,

Affirming the need to promote active international cooperation among the States concerned before, during and after an accident, to enhance appropriate policies and to reinforce and coordinate action at all appropriate levels for promoting the prevention of, preparedness for and response to the transboundary effects of industrial accidents,

Noting the importance and usefulness of bilateral and multilateral arrangements for the prevention of, preparedness for and response to the effects of industrial accidents,

Conscious of the role played in this respect by the United Nations Economic Commission for Europe (ECE) and recalling, *inter alia*, the ECE Code of Conduct on Accidental Pollution of Transboundary Inland Waters and the Convention on Environmental Impact Assessment in a Transboundary Context,

Having regard to the relevant provisions of the Final Act of the Conference on Security and Cooperation in Europe (CSCE), the Concluding Document of the Vienna Meeting of Representatives of the Participating States of the CSCE, and the outcome of the Sofia Meeting on the Protection of the Environment of the CSCE, as well as to pertinent activities and mechanisms in the United Nations Environment Programme (UNEP), in particular the APELL programme, in the International Labour Organisation (ILO), in particular the Code of Practice on the Prevention of Major Industrial Accidents, and in other relevant international organizations,

Considering the pertinent provisions of the Declaration of the United Nations Conference on the Human En-

vironment, and in particular principle 21, according to which States have, in accordance with the Charter of the United Nations and the principles of international law, the sovereign right to exploit their own resources pursuant to their own environmental policies, and the responsibility to ensure that activities within their jurisdiction or control do not cause damage to the environment of other States or of areas beyond the limits of national jurisdiction,

Taking account of the polluter-pays principle as a general principle of international environmental law,

Underlining the principles of international law and custom, in particular the principles of good-neighbourliness, reciprocity, non-discrimination and good faith,

Have agreed as follows:

Article 1

DEFINITIONS

For the purposes of this Convention,

(*a*) "Industrial accident" means an event resulting from an uncontrolled development in the course of any activity involving hazardous substances either:

(i) In an installation, for example during manufacture, use, storage, handling, or disposal; or

(ii) During transportation in so far as it is covered by paragraph 2(*d*) of Article 2;

(*b*) "Hazardous activity" means any activity in which one or more hazardous substances are present or may be present in quantities at or in excess of the threshold quantities listed in Annex I hereto, and which is capable of causing transboundary effects;

(*c*) "Effects" means any direct or indirect, immediate or delayed adverse consequences caused by an industrial accident on, *inter alia*:

(i) Human beings, flora and fauna;

(ii) Soil, water, air and landscape;

(iii) The interaction between the factors in (i) and (ii);

(iv) Material assets and cultural heritage, including historical monuments;

(*d*) "Transboundary effects" means serious effects within the jurisdiction of a Party as a result of an industrial accident occurring within the jurisdiction of another Party;

(*e*) "Operator" means any natural or legal person, including public authorities, in charge of an activity, e.g. supervising, planning to carry out or carrying out an activity;

(*f*) "Party" means, unless the text otherwise indicates, a Contracting Party to this Convention;

(*g*) "Party of origin" means any Party or Parties under whose jurisdiction an industrial accident occurs or is capable of occurring;

(*h*) "Affected Party" means any Party or Parties affected or capable of being affected by transboundary effects of an industrial accident;

(*i*) "Parties concerned" means any Party of origin and any affected Party;

(*j*) "The public" means one or more natural or legal persons.

Article 2

SCOPE

1. This Convention shall apply to the prevention of, preparedness for and response to industrial accidents capable of causing transboundary effects, including the effects of such accidents caused by natural disasters, and to international cooperation concerning mutual assistance, research and development, exchange of information and exchange of technology in the area of prevention of, preparedness for and response to industrial accidents.

2. This Convention shall not apply to:

(*a*) Nuclear accidents or radiological emergencies;

(*b*) Accidents at military installations;

(*c*) Dam failures, with the exception of the effects of industrial accidents caused by such failures;

(*d*) Land-based transport accidents with the exception of:

(i) Emergency response to such accidents;

(ii) Transportation on the site of the hazardous activity;

(*e*) Accidental release of genetically modified organisms;

(*f*) Accidents caused by activities in the marine environment, including seabed exploration or exploitation;

(*g*) Spills of oil or other harmful substances at sea.

Article 3

GENERAL PROVISIONS

1. The Parties shall, taking into account efforts already made at national and international levels, take appropriate measures and cooperate within the framework of this Convention, to protect human beings and the environment against industrial accidents by preventing such accidents as far as possible, by reducing their frequency and severity and by mitigating their effects. To this end, preventive, preparedness and response measures, including restoration measures, shall be applied.

2. The Parties shall, by means of exchange of information, consultation and other cooperative measures and without undue delay, develop and implement policies and strategies for reducing the risks of industrial accidents and improving preventive, preparedness and response measures, including restoration measures, taking into account, in order to avoid unnecessary duplication, efforts already made at national and international levels.

3. The Parties shall ensure that the operator is obliged to take all measures necessary for the safe performance of the hazardous activity and for the prevention of industrial accidents.

4. To implement the provisions of this Convention, the Parties shall take appropriate legislative, regulatory, administrative and financial measures for the prevention of, preparedness for and response to industrial accidents.

5. The provisions of this Convention shall not prejudice any obligations of the Parties under international law with regard to industrial accidents and hazardous activities.

Article 4

IDENTIFICATION, CONSULTATION AND ADVICE

1. For the purpose of undertaking preventive measures and setting up preparedness measures, the Party of origin shall take measures, as appropriate, to identify hazardous activities within its jurisdiction and to ensure that affected Parties are notified of any such proposed or existing activity.

2. Parties concerned shall, at the initiative of any such Party, enter into discussions on the identification of those hazardous activities that are, reasonably, capable of causing transboundary effects. If the Parties concerned do not agree on whether an activity is such a hazardous activity, any such Party may, unless the Parties concerned agree on another method of resolving the question, submit that question to an inquiry commission in accordance with the provisions of Annex II hereto for advice.

3. The Parties shall, with respect to proposed or existing hazardous activities, apply the procedures set out in Annex III hereto.

4. When a hazardous activity is subject to an environmental impact assessment in accordance with the Convention on Environmental Impact Assessment in a Transboundary Context and that assessment includes an evaluation of the transboundary effects of industrial accidents from the hazardous activity which is performed in conformity with the terms of this Convention, the final decision taken for the purposes of the Convention on En-

vironmental Impact Assessment in a Transboundary Context shall fulfil the relevant requirements of this Convention.

Article 5

VOLUNTARY EXTENSION

Parties concerned should, at the initiative of any of them, enter into discussions on whether to treat an activity not covered by Annex I as a hazardous activity. Upon mutual agreement, they may use an advisory mechanism of their choice, or an inquiry commission in accordance with Annex II, to advise them. Where the Parties concerned so agree, this Convention, or any part thereof, shall apply to the activity in question as if it were a hazardous activity.

Article 6

PREVENTION

1. The Parties shall take appropriate measures for the prevention of industrial accidents, including measures to induce action by operators to reduce the risk of industrial accidents. Such measures may include, but are not limited to those referred to in Annex IV hereto.

2. With regard to any hazardous activity, the Party of origin shall require the operator to demonstrate the safe performance of the hazardous activity by the provision of information such as basic details of the process, including but not limited to, analysis and evaluation as detailed in Annex V hereto.

Article 7

DECISION-MAKING ON SITING

Within the framework of its legal system, the Party of origin shall, with the objective of minimizing the risk to the population and the environment of all affected Parties, seek the establishment of policies on the siting of new hazardous activities and on significant modifications to existing hazardous activities. Within the framework of their legal systems, the affected Parties shall seek the establishment of policies on significant developments in areas which could be affected by transboundary effects of an industrial accident arising out of a hazardous activity so as to minimize the risks involved. In elaborating and establishing these policies, the Parties should consider the matters set out in Annex V, paragraph 2, subparagraphs (1) to (8), and Annex VI hereto.

Article 8

EMERGENCY PREPAREDNESS

1. The Parties shall take appropriate measures to establish and maintain adequate emergency preparedness to respond to industrial accidents. The Parties shall ensure that preparedness measures are taken to mitigate transboundary effects of such accidents, on-site duties being undertaken by operators. These measures may include, but are not limited to those referred to in Annex VII hereto. In particular, the Parties concerned shall inform each other of their contingency plans.

2. The Party of origin shall ensure for hazardous activities the preparation and implementation of on-site contingency plans, including suitable measures for response and other measures to prevent and minimize transboundary effects. The Party of origin shall provide to the other Parties concerned the elements it has for the elaboration of contingency plans.

3. Each Party shall ensure for hazardous activities the preparation and implementation of off-site contingency plans covering measures to be taken within its territory to prevent and minimize transboundary effects. In preparing these plans, account shall be taken of the conclusions of analysis and evaluation, in particular the matters set out in Annex V, paragraph 2, subparagraphs (1) to (5). Parties concerned shall endeavour to make such plans compatible. Where appropriate, joint off-site contingency plans shall be drawn up in order to facilitate the adoption of adequate response measures.

4. Contingency plans should be reviewed regularly, or when circumstances so require, taking into account the experience gained in dealing with actual emergencies.

Article 9

INFORMATION TO, AND PARTICIPATION OF THE PUBLIC

1. The Parties shall ensure that adequate information is given to the public in the areas capable of being affected by an industrial accident arising out of a hazardous activity. This information shall be transmitted through such channels as the Parties deem appropriate, shall include the elements contained in Annex VIII hereto and should take into account matters set out in Annex V, paragraph 2, subparagraphs (1) to (4) and (9).

2. The Party of origin shall, in accordance with the provisions of this Convention and whenever possible and appropriate, give the public in the areas capable of being affected an opportunity to participate in relevant procedures with the aim of making known its views and concerns on prevention and preparedness measures, and shall ensure that the opportunity given to the public of the affected Party is equivalent to that given to the public of the Party of origin.

3. The Parties shall, in accordance with their legal systems and, if desired, on a reciprocal basis provide

natural or legal persons who are being or are capable of being adversely affected by the transboundary effects of an industrial accident in the territory of a Party, with access to, and treatment in the relevant administrative and judicial proceedings, including the possibilities of starting a legal action and appealing a decision affecting their rights, equivalent to those available to persons within their own jurisdiction.

Article 10

INDUSTRIAL ACCIDENT NOTIFICATION SYSTEMS

1. The Parties shall, with the aim of obtaining and transmitting industrial accident notifications containing information needed to counteract transboundary effects, provide for the establishment and operation of compatible and efficient industrial accident notification systems at appropriate levels.

2. In the event of an industrial accident, or imminent threat thereof, which causes or is capable of causing transboundary effects, the Party of origin shall ensure that affected Parties are, without delay, notified at appropriate levels through the industrial accident notification systems. Such notification shall include the elements contained in Annex IX hereto.

3. The Parties concerned shall ensure that, in the event of an industrial accident or imminent threat thereof, the contingency plans prepared in accordance with Article 8 are activated as soon as possible and to the extent appropriate to the circumstances.

Article 11

RESPONSE

1. The Parties shall ensure that, in the event of an industrial accident, or imminent threat thereof, adequate response measures are taken, as soon as possible and using the most efficient practices, to contain and minimize effects.

2. In the event of an industrial accident, or imminent threat thereof, which causes or is capable of causing transboundary effects, the Parties concerned shall ensure that the effects are assessed—where appropriate, jointly for the purpose of taking adequate response measures. The Parties concerned shall endeavour to coordinate their response measures.

Article 12

MUTUAL ASSISTANCE

1. If a Party needs assistance in the event of an industrial accident, it may ask for assistance from other Parties, indicating the scope and type of assistance required. A Party to whom a request for assistance is directed shall promptly decide and inform the requesting Party whether it is in a position to render the assistance required and indicate the scope and terms of the assistance that might be rendered.

2. The Parties concerned shall cooperate to facilitate the prompt provision of assistance agreed to under paragraph 1 of this Article, including, where appropriate, action to minimize the consequences and effects of the industrial accident, and to provide general assistance. Where Parties do not have bilateral or multilateral agreements which cover their arrangements for providing mutual assistance, the assistance shall be rendered in accordance with Annex X hereto, unless the Parties agree otherwise.

Article 13

RESPONSIBILITY AND LIABILITY

The Parties shall support appropriate international efforts to elaborate rules, criteria and procedures in the field of responsibility and liability.

Article 14

RESEARCH AND DEVELOPMENT

The Parties shall, as appropriate, initiate and cooperate in the conduct of research into, and in the development of methods and technologies for the prevention of, preparedness for and response to industrial accidents. For these purposes, the Parties shall encourage and actively promote scientific and technological cooperation, including research into less hazardous processes aimed at limiting accident hazards and preventing and limiting the consequences of industrial accidents.

Article 15

EXCHANGE OF INFORMATION

The Parties shall, at the multilateral or bilateral level, exchange reasonably obtainable information, including the elements contained in Annex XI hereto.

Article 16

EXCHANGE OF TECHNOLOGY

1. The Parties shall, consistent with their laws, regulations and practices, facilitate the exchange of technology for the prevention of, preparedness for and response to the effects of industrial accidents, particularly through the promotion of:

(a) Exchange of available technology on various financial bases;

(b) Direct industrial contacts and cooperation;

(c) Exchange of information and experience;

(*d*) Provision of technical assistance.

2. In promoting the activities specified in paragraph 1, subparagraphs (*a*) to (*d*) of this Article, the Parties shall create favourable conditions by facilitating contacts and cooperation among appropriate organizations and individuals in both the private and the public sectors that are capable of providing technology, design and engineering services, equipment or finance.

Article 17

COMPETENT AUTHORITIES AND POINTS OF CONTACT

1. Each Party shall designate or establish one or more competent authorities for the purposes of this Convention.

2. Without prejudice to other arrangements at the bilateral or multilateral level, each Party shall designate or establish one point of contact for the purpose of industrial accident notifications pursuant to Article 10, and one point of contact for the purpose of mutual assistance pursuant to Article 12. These points of contact should preferably be the same.

3. Each Party shall, within three months of the date of entry into force of this Convention for that Party, inform the other Parties, through the secretariat referred to in Article 20, which body or bodies it has designated as its point(s) of contact and as its competent authority or authorities.

4. Each Party shall, within one month of the date of decision, inform the other Parties, through the secretariat, of any changes regarding the designation(s) it has made under paragraph 3 of this Article.

5. Each Party shall keep its point of contact and industrial accident notification systems pursuant to Article 10 operational at all times.

6. Each Party shall keep its point of contact and the authorities responsible for making and receiving requests for, and accepting offers of assistance pursuant to Article 12 operational at all times.

Article 18

CONFERENCE OF THE PARTIES

1. The representatives of the Parties shall constitute the Conference of the Parties of this Convention and hold their meetings on a regular basis. The first meeting of the Conference of the Parties shall be convened not later than one year after the date of the entry into force of this Convention. Thereafter, a meeting of the Conference of the Parties shall be held at least once a year or at the written request of any Party, provided that, within six months of the request being communicated to them by the secretariat, it is supported by at least one third of the Parties.

2. The Conference of the Parties shall:

(*a*) Review the implementation of this Convention;

(*b*) Carry out advisory functions aimed at strengthening the ability of Parties to prevent, prepare for and respond to the transboundary effects of industrial accidents, and at facilitating the provision of technical assistance and advice at the request of Parties faced with industrial accidents;

(*c*) Establish, as appropriate, working groups and other appropriate mechanisms to consider matters related to the implementation and development of this Convention and, to this end, to prepare appropriate studies and other documentation and submit recommendations for consideration by the Conference of the Parties;

(*d*) Fulfil such other functions as may be appropriate under the provisions of this Convention;

(*e*) At its first meeting, consider and, by consensus, adopt rules of procedure for its meetings.

3. The Conference of the Parties, in discharging its functions, shall, when it deems appropriate, also cooperate with other relevant international organizations.

4. The Conference of the Parties shall, at its first meeting, establish a programme of work, in particular with regard to the items contained in Annex XII hereto. The Conference of the Parties shall also decide on the method of work, including the use of national centres and cooperation with relevant international organizations and the establishment of a system with a view to facilitating the implementation of this Convention, in particular for mutual assistance in the event of an industrial accident, and building upon pertinent existing activities within relevant international organizations. As part of the programme of work, the Conference of the Parties shall review existing national, regional and international centres, and other bodies and programmes aimed at coordinating information and efforts in the prevention of, preparedness for and response to industrial accidents, with a view to determining what additional international institutions or centres may be needed to carry out the tasks listed in Annex XII.

5. The Conference of the Parties shall, at its first meeting, commence consideration of procedures to create more favourable conditions for the exchange of technology for the prevention of, preparedness for and response to the effects of industrial accidents.

6. The Conference of the Parties shall adopt guidelines and criteria to facilitate the identification of hazardous activities for the purposes of this Convention.

Article 19

RIGHT TO VOTE

1. Except as provided for in paragraph 2 of this Article, each Party to this Convention shall have one vote.

2. Regional economic integration organizations as defined in Article 27 shall, in matters within their competence, exercise their right to vote with a number of

votes equal to the number of their member States which are Parties to this Convention. Such organizations shall not exercise their right to vote if their member States exercise theirs, and vice versa.

Article 20

SECRETARIAT

The Executive Secretary of the Economic Commission for Europe shall carry out the following secretariat functions:

(a) Convene and prepare meetings of the Parties;

(b) Transmit to the Parties reports and other information received in accordance with the provisions of this Convention;

(c) Such other functions as may be determined by the Parties.

Article 21

SETTLEMENT OF DISPUTES

1. If a dispute arises between two or more Parties about the interpretation or application of this Convention, they shall seek a solution by negotiation or by any other method of dispute settlement acceptable to the parties to the dispute.

2. When signing, ratifying, accepting, approving or acceding to this Convention, or at any time thereafter, a Party may declare in writing to the Depositary that, for a dispute not resolved in accordance with paragraph 1 of this Article, it accepts one or both of the following means of dispute settlement as compulsory in relation to any Party accepting the same obligation:

(a) Submission of the dispute to the International Court of Justice;

(b) Arbitration in accordance with the procedure set out in Annex XIII hereto.

3. If the parties to the dispute have accepted both means of dispute settlement referred to in paragraph 2 of this Article, the dispute may be submitted only to the International Court of Justice, unless the parties to the dispute agree otherwise.

Article 22

LIMITATIONS ON THE SUPPLY OF INFORMATION

1. The provisions of this Convention shall not affect the rights or the obligations of Parties in accordance with their national laws, regulations, administrative provisions or accepted legal practices and applicable international regulations to protect information related to personal data, industrial and commercial secrecy, including intellectual property, or national security.

2. If a Party nevertheless decides to supply such protected information to another Party, the Party receiving such protected information shall respect the confidentiality of the information received and the conditions under which it is supplied, and shall only use that information for the purposes for which it was supplied.

Article 23

IMPLEMENTATION

The Parties shall report periodically on the implementation of this Convention.

Article 24

BILATERAL AND MULTILATERAL AGREEMENTS

1. The Parties may, in order to implement their obligations under this Convention, continue existing or enter into new bilateral or multilateral agreements or other arrangements.

2. The provisions of this Convention shall not affect the right of Parties to take, by bilateral or multilateral agreement where appropriate, more stringent measures than those required by this Convention.

Article 25

STATUS OF ANNEXES

The Annexes to this Convention form an integral part of the Convention.

Article 26

AMENDMENTS TO THE CONVENTION

1. Any Party may propose amendments to this Convention.

2. The text of any proposed amendment to this Convention shall be submitted in writing to the Executive Secretary of the Economic Commission for Europe, who shall circulate it to all Parties. The Conference of the Parties shall discuss proposed amendments at its next annual meeting, provided that such proposals have been circulated to the Parties by the Executive Secretary of the Economic Commission for Europe at least ninety days in advance.

3. For amendments to this Convention—other than those to Annex I, for which the procedure is described in paragraph 4 of this Article:

(a) Amendments shall be adopted by consensus of the Parties present at the meeting and shall be submitted by the Depositary to all Parties for ratification, acceptance or approval;

(*b*) Instruments of ratification, acceptance or approval of amendments shall be deposited with the Depositary. Amendments adopted in accordance with this Article shall enter into force for Parties that have accepted them on the ninetieth day following the day of receipt by the Depositary of the sixteenth instrument of ratification, acceptance or approval;

(*c*) Thereafter, amendments shall enter into force for any other Party on the ninetieth day after that Party deposits its instruments of ratification, acceptance or approval of the amendments.

4.   For amendments to Annex I:

(*a*) The Parties shall make every effort to reach agreement by consensus. If all efforts at consensus have been exhausted and no agreement reached, the amendments shall, as a last resort, be adopted by a nine-tenths majority vote of the Parties present and voting at the meeting. If adopted by the Conference of the Parties, the amendments shall be communicated to the Parties and recommended for approval;

(*b*) On the expiry of twelve months from the date of their communication by the Executive Secretary of the Economic Commission for Europe, the amendments to Annex I shall become effective for those Parties to this Convention which have not submitted a notification in accordance with the provisions of paragraph 4 (*c*) of this Article, provided that at least sixteen Parties have not submitted such a notification;

(*c*) Any Party that is unable to approve an amendment to Annex I of this Convention shall so notify the Executive Secretary of the Economic Commission for Europe in writing within twelve months from the date of the communication of the adoption. The Executive Secretary shall without delay notify all Parties of any such notification received. A Party may at any time substitute an acceptance for its previous notification and the amendment to Annex I shall thereupon enter into force for that Party.

(*d*) For the purpose of this paragraph ''Parties present and voting'' means Parties present and casting an affirmative or negative vote.

Article 27

SIGNATURE

This Convention shall be open for signature at Helsinki from 17 to 18 March 1992 inclusive, and thereafter at United Nations Headquarters in New York until 18 September 1992, by States members of the Economic Commission for Europe, as well as States having consultative status with the Economic Commission for Europe pursuant to paragraph 8 of Economic and Social Council resolution 36 (IV) of 28 March 1947, and by regional economic integration organizations constituted by sovereign States members of the Economic Commission for Europe to which their member States have transferred competence in respect of matters governed by this Con-

vention, including the competence to enter into treaties in respect of these matters.

Article 28

DEPOSITARY

The Secretary-General of the United Nations shall act as the Depositary of this Convention.

Article 29

RATIFICATION, ACCEPTANCE, APPROVAL AND ACCESSION

1.   This Convention shall be subject to ratification, acceptance or approval by the signatory States and regional economic integration organizations referred to in Article 27.

2.   This Convention shall be open for accession by the States and organizations referred to in Article 27.

3.   Any organization referred to in Article 27 which becomes Party to this Convention without any of its member States being a Party shall be bound by all the obligations under this Convention. In the case of such organizations, one or more of whose member States is a Party to this Convention, the organization and its member States shall decide on their respective responsibilities for the performance of their obligations under this Convention. In such cases, the organization and the member States shall not be entitled to exercise rights under this Convention concurrently.

4.   In their instruments of ratification, acceptance, approval or accession, the regional economic integration organizations referred to in Article 27 shall declare the extent of their competence with respect to the matters governed by this Convention. These organizations shall also inform the Depositary of any substantial modification to the extent of their competence.

Article 30

ENTRY INTO FORCE

1.   This Convention shall enter into force on the ninetieth day after the date of deposit of the sixteenth instrument of ratification, acceptance, approval or accession.

2.   For the purposes of paragraph 1 of this Article, any instrument deposited by an organization referred to in Article 27 shall not be counted as additional to those deposited by States members of such an organization.

3.   For each State or organization referred to in Article 27 which ratifies, accepts or approves this Convention or accedes thereto after the deposit of the sixteenth instrument of ratification, acceptance, approval or accession, this Convention shall enter into force on the nineti-

eth day after the date of deposit by such State or organization of its instrument of ratification, acceptance, approval or accession.

Article 31

WITHDRAWAL

1. At any time after three years from the date on which this Convention has come into force with respect to a Party, that Party may withdraw from this Convention by giving written notification to the Depositary. Any such withdrawal shall take effect on the ninetieth day after the date of the receipt of the notification by the Depositary.

2. Any such withdrawal shall not affect the application of Article 4 to an activity in respect of which a notification has been made pursuant to Article 4, paragraph 1, or a request for discussions has been made pursuant to Article 4, paragraph 2.

Article 32

AUTHENTIC TEXTS

The original of this Convention, of which the English, French and Russian texts are equally authentic, shall be deposited with the Secretary-General of the United Nations.

IN WITNESS WHEREOF the undersigned, being duly authorized thereto, have signed this Convention.

DONE at Helsinki, this seventeenth day of March one thousand nine hundred and ninety-two.

ANNEXES

ANNEX I

Hazardous substances for the purposes of defining hazardous activities

The quantities set out below relate to each activity or group of activities. Where a range of quantities is given in Part I, the threshold quantities are the maximum quantities given in each range. Five years after the entry into force of this Convention, the lowest quantity given in each range shall become the threshold quantity, unless amended.

Where a substance or preparation named in Part II also falls within a category in Part I, the threshold quantity set out in Part II shall be used.

For the identification of hazardous activities, Parties shall take into consideration the foreseeable possibility of aggravation of the hazards involved and the quantities of the hazardous substances and their proximity, whether under the charge of one or more operators.

PART I. *Categories of substances and preparations not specifically named in Part II*

Category	Threshold Quantity (Tonnes)
1. Flammable gases[1(a)] including LPG	200
2. Highly flammable liquids[1(b)]	50,000
3. Very toxic[1(c)]	20
4. Toxic[1(d)]	500-200
5. Oxidizing[1(e)]	500-200
6. Explosive[1(f)]	200-50
7. Flammable liquids[1(g)] (handled under special conditions of pressure and temperature)	200
8. Dangerous for the environment[1(h)]	200

PART II. *Named substances*

Substance	Threshold Quantity (Tonnes)
1. Ammonia	500
2 a Ammonium nitrate[2]	2,500
b Ammonium nitrate in the form of fertilizers[3]	10,000
3. Acrylonitrile	200
4. Chlorine	25
5. Ethylene oxide	50
6. Hydrogen cyanide	20
7. Hydrogen fluoride	50
8. Hydrogen sulphide	50
9. Sulphur dioxide	250
10. Sulphur trioxide	75
11. Lead alkyls	50
12. Phosgene	0.75
13. Methyl isocyanate	0.15

NOTES

1. *Indicative criteria*. In the absence of other appropriate criteria, Parties may use the following criteria when classifying substances or preparations for the purposes of Part I of this Annex.

(a) FLAMMABLE GASES: substances which in the gaseous state at normal pressure and mixed with air become flammable and the boiling point of which at normal pressure is 20°C or below.

(b) HIGHLY FLAMMABLE LIQUIDS: substances which have a flash point lower than 21°C and the boiling point of which at normal pressure is above 20°C.

(c) VERY TOXIC: substances with properties corresponding to those in table 1 or table 2 below, and which, owing to their physical and chemical properties, are capable of creating industrial accident hazards.

(Note 1 (c) continued on next page.)

(Note 1 (c) continued.)

TABLE 1

$LD_{50}(oral)(1)$ mg/kg body weight $LD_{50} \leq 25$	$LD_{50}(dermal)(2)$ mg/kg body weight $LD_{50} \leq 50$	$LC_{50}(3)$ mg/l (inhalation) $LC_{50} \leq 0.5$

(1) LD_{50} oral in rats.
(2) LD_{50} dermal in rats or rabbits.
(3) LC_{50} by inhalation (four hours) in rats.

TABLE 2

Discriminating dose mg/kg body weight	< 5

where the acute oral toxicity in animals of the substance has been determined using the fixed-dose procedure.

(d) TOXIC: substances with properties corresponding to those in table 3 or 4 and having physical and chemical properties capable of creating industrial accident hazards.

TABLE 3

$LD_{50}(oral)(1)$ mg/kg body weight $25 < LD_{50} \leq 200$	$LD_{50}(dermal)(2)$ mg/kg body weight $50 < LD_{50} \leq 400$	$LC_{50}(3)$ mg/l(inhalation) $0.5 < LC_{50} \leq 2$

(1) LD_{50} oral in rats.
(2) LD_{50} dermal in rats or rabbits.
(3) LC_{50} by inhalation (four hours) in rats.

TABLE 4

Discriminating dose mg/kg body weight	$= 5$

where the acute oral toxicity in animals of the substance has been determined using the fixed-dose procedure.

(e) OXIDIZING: substances which give rise to highly exothermic reaction when in contact with other substances, particularly flammable substances.

(f) EXPLOSIVE: substances which may explode under the effect of flame or which are more sensitive to shocks or friction than dinitrobenzene.

(g) FLAMMABLE LIQUIDS: substances which have a flash point lower than 55°C and which remain liquid under pressure, where particular processing conditions, such as high pressure and high temperature, may create industrial accident hazards.

(h) DANGEROUS FOR THE ENVIRONMENT: substances showing the values for acute toxicity to the aquatic environment corresponding to table 5.

TABLE 5

$LC_{50}(1)$ mg/l $LC_{50} \leq 10$	$EC_{50}(2)$ mg/l $EC_{50} \leq 10$	$IC_{50}(3)$ mg/l $IC_{50} \leq 10$

(1) LC_{50} fish (96 hours).
(2) EC_{50} daphnia (48 hours).
(3) IC_{50} algae (72 hours).

where the substance is not readily degradable, or the log Pow > 3.0 (unless the experimentally determined BCF < 100).

(i) LD - lethal dose.
(j) LC - lethal concentration.
(k) EC - effective concentration.
(l) IC - inhibiting concentration.
(m) Pow - partition coefficient octanol/water.
(n) BCF - bioconcentration factor.

2. This applies to ammonium nitrate and mixtures of ammonium nitrate where the nitrogen content derived from the ammonium nitrate is > 28% by weight, and to aqueous solutions of ammonium nitrate where the concentration of ammonium nitrate is > 90% by weight.

3. This applies to straight ammonium nitrate fertilizers and to compound fertilizers where the nitrogen content derived from the ammonium nitrate is > 28% by weight (a compound fertilizer contains ammonium nitrate together with phosphate and/or potash).

4. Mixtures and preparations containing such substances shall be treated in the same way as the pure substance unless they no longer exhibit equivalent properties and are not capable of producing transboundary effects.

ANNEX II

Inquiry commission procedure pursuant to Articles 4 and 5

1. The requesting Party or Parties shall notify the secretariat that it or they is (are) submitting question(s) to an inquiry commission established in accordance with the provisions of this Annex. The notification shall state the subject-matter of the inquiry. The secretariat shall immediately inform all Parties to the Convention of this submission.

2. The inquiry commission shall consist of three members. Both the requesting party and the other party to the inquiry procedure shall appoint a scientific or technical expert and the two experts so appointed shall designate by common agreement a third expert, who shall be the president of the inquiry commission. The latter shall not be a national of one of the parties to the inquiry procedure, nor have his or her usual place of residence in the territory of one of these parties, nor be employed by any of them, nor have dealt with the case in any other capacity.

3. If the president of the inquiry commission has not been designated within two months of the appointment of the second expert, the Executive Secretary of the Economic Commission for Europe shall, at the request of either party, designate the president within a further two-month period.

4. If one of the parties to the inquiry procedure does not appoint an expert within one month of its receipt of the notification by the secretariat, the other party may inform the Executive Secretary of the Economic Commission for Europe, who shall designate the president of the inquiry commission within a further two-month period. Upon designation, the president of the inquiry commission shall request the party which has not appointed an expert to do so within one month. If it fails to do so within that period, the president shall inform the Executive Secretary of the Economic Commission for Europe who shall make this appointment within a further two-month period.

5. The inquiry commission shall adopt its own rules of procedure.

6. The inquiry commission may take all appropriate measures in order to carry out its functions.

7. The parties to the inquiry procedure shall facilitate the work of the inquiry commission and in particular shall, using all means at their disposal:

(a) Provide the inquiry commission with all relevant documents, facilities and information;

(b) Enable the inquiry commission, where necessary, to call witnesses or experts and receive their evidence.

8. The parties and the experts shall protect the confidentiality of any information they receive in confidence during the work of the inquiry commission.

9. If one of the parties to the inquiry procedure does not appear before the inquiry commission or fails to present its case, the other party may request the inquiry commission to continue the proceedings and to complete its work. Absence of a party or failure of a party to present its case shall not constitute a bar to the continuation and completion of the work of the inquiry commission.

10. Unless the inquiry commission determines otherwise because of the particular circumstances of the matter, the expenses of the inquiry commission, including the remuneration of its members, shall be borne equally by the parties to the inquiry procedure. The inquiry commission shall keep a record of all its expenses and shall furnish a final statement thereof to the parties.

11. Any Party which has an interest of a factual nature in the subject-matter of the inquiry procedure and which may be affected by an opinion in the matter may intervene in the proceedings with the consent of the inquiry commission.

12. The decisions of the inquiry commission on matters of the procedure shall be taken by majority vote of its members. The final opinion of the inquiry commission shall reflect the view of the majority of its members and shall include any dissenting view.

13. The inquiry commission shall present its final opinion within two months of the date on which it was established, unless it finds it necessary to extend this time-limit for a period which should not exceed two months.

14. The final opinion of the inquiry commission shall be based on accepted scientific principles. The final opinion shall be transmitted by the inquiry commission to the parties to the inquiry procedure and to the secretariat.

ANNEX III

Procedures pursuant to Article 4

1. A Party of origin may request consultations with another Party, in accordance with paragraphs 2 to 5 of this Annex, in order to determine whether that Party is an affected Party.

2. For a proposed or existing hazardous activity, the Party of origin shall, for the purposes of ensuring adequate and effective consultations, provide for the notification at appropriate levels of any Party that it considers may be an an affected Party as early as possible and no later than when informing its own public about that proposed or existing activity. For existing hazardous activities such notification shall be provided no later than two years after the entry into force of this Convention for a Party of origin.

3. The notification shall contain, *inter alia*:

(*a*) Information on the hazardous activity, including any available information or report, such as information produced in accordance with Article 6, on its possible transboundary effects in the event of an industrial accident;

(*b*) An indication of a reasonable time within which a response under paragraph 4 of this Annex is required, taking into account the nature of the activity;

and may include the information set out in paragraph 6 of this Annex.

4. The notified Parties shall respond to the Party of origin within the time specified in the notification, acknowledging receipt of the notification and indicating whether they intend to enter into consultation.

5. If a notified Party indicates that it does not intend to enter into consultation, or if it does not respond within the time specified in the notification, the provisions set down in the following paragraphs of this Annex shall not apply. In such circumstances, the right of a Party of origin to determine whether to carry out an assessment and analysis on the basis of its national law and practice is not prejudiced.

6. Upon receipt of a response from a notified Party indicating its desire to enter into consultation, the Party of origin shall, if it has not already done so, provide to the notified Party:

(*a*) Relevant information regarding the time schedule for analysis, including an indication of the time schedule for the transmittal of comments;

(*b*) Relevant information on the hazardous activity and its transboundary effects in the event of an industrial accident;

(*c*) The opportunity to participate in evaluations of the information or any report demonstrating possible transboundary effects.

7. An affected Party shall, at the request of the Party of origin, provide the latter with reasonably obtainable information relating to the area under the jurisdiction of the affected Party capable of being affected, where such information is necessary for the preparation of the assessment and analysis and measures. The information shall be furnished promptly and, as appropriate, through a joint body where one exists.

8. The Party of origin shall furnish the affected Party directly, as appropriate, or, where one exists, through a joint body with the analysis and evaluation documentation as described in Annex V, paragraphs 1 and 2.

9. The Parties concerned shall inform the public in areas reasonably capable of being affected by the hazardous activity and shall arrange for the distribution of the analysis and evaluation documentation to it and to authorities in the relevant areas. The Parties shall ensure them an opportunity for making comments on, or objections to, the hazardous activity and shall arrange for their views to be submitted to the competent authority of the Party of origin, either directly to that authority or, where appropriate, through the Party of origin, within a reasonable time.

10. The Party of origin shall, after completion of the analysis and evaluation documentation, enter without undue delay into consultations with the affected Party concerning, *inter alia*, the transboundary effects of the hazardous activity in the event of an industrial accident, and measures to reduce or eliminate its effects. The consultations may relate to:

(*a*) Possible alternatives to the hazardous activity, including the no-action alternative, and possible measures to mitigate transboundary effects at the expense of the Party of origin;

(*b*) Other forms of possible mutual assistance for reducing any transboundary effects;

(*c*) Any other appropriate matters.

The Parties concerned shall, on the commencement of such consultations, agree on a reasonable time-frame for the duration of the consultation period. Any such consultations may be conducted through an appropriate joint body, where one exists.

11. The Parties concerned shall ensure that due account is taken of the analysis and evaluation, as well as of the comments received pursuant to paragraph 9 of this Annex and of the outcome of the consultations referred to in paragraph 10 of this Annex.

12. The Party of origin shall notify the affected Parties of any decision on the activity, along with the reasons and considerations on which it was based.

13. If, after additional and relevant information concerning the transboundary effects of a hazardous activity and which was not available at the time consultations were held with respect to that activity, becomes available to a Party concerned, that Party shall immediately inform the other Party or Parties concerned. If one of the Parties concerned so requests, renewed consultations shall be held.

ANNEX IV

Preventive measures pursuant to Article 6

The following measures may be carried out, depending on national laws and practices, by Parties, competent authorities, operators, or by joint efforts:

1. The setting of general or specific safety objectives;

2. The adoption of legislative provisions or guidelines concerning safety measures and safety standards;

3. The identification of those hazardous activities which require special preventive measures, which may include a licensing or authorization system;

4. The evaluation of risk analyses or of safety studies for hazardous activities and an action plan for the implementation of necessary measures;

5. The provision to the competent authorities of the information needed to assess risks;

6. The application of the most appropriate technology in order to prevent industrial accidents and protect human beings and the environment;

7. The undertaking, in order to prevent industrial accidents, of the appropriate education and training of all persons engaged in hazardous activities on-site under both normal and abnormal conditions;

8. The establishment of internal managerial structures and practices designed to implement and maintain safety regulations effectively;

9. The monitoring and auditing of hazardous activities and the carrying out of inspections.

ANNEX V

Analysis and evaluation

1. The analysis and evaluation of the hazardous activity should be performed with a scope and to a depth which vary depending on the purpose for which they are carried out.

2. The following table illustrates, for the purposes of the related Articles, matters which should be considered in the analysis and evaluation, for the purposes listed:

Purpose of analysis	Matters to be considered
Emergency planning under Article 8	(1) The quantities and properties of hazardous substances on the site;
	(2) Brief descriptive scenarios of a representative sample of industrial accidents possibly arising from the hazardous activity, including an indication of the likelihood of each;
	(3) For each scenario:
	(*a*) The approximate quantity of a release;
	(*b*) The extent and severity of the resulting consequences both for people and for the non-human environment in favourable and unfavourable conditions, including the extent of resulting hazard zones;
	(*c*) The time-scale within which the industrial accident could develop from the initiating event;
	(*d*) Any action which could be taken to minimize the likelihood of escalation.
	(4) The size and distribution of the population in the vicinity, including any large concentrations of people potentially in the hazard zone;
	(5) The age, mobility and susceptibility of that population.

Purpose of analysis	*Matters to be considered*
	In addition to items (1) to (5) above:
Decision-making on siting under Article 7	(6) The severity of the harm inflicted on people and the environment, depending on the nature and circumstances of the release;
	(7) The distance from the location of the hazardous activity at which harmful effects on people and the environment may reasonably occur in the event of an industrial accident;
	(8) The same information not only for the present situation but also for planned or reasonably foreseeable future developments.
Information to the public under Article 9	In addition to items (1) to (4) above:
	(9) The people who may be affected by an industrial accident.
Preventive measures under Article 6	In addition to items (4) to (9) above, more detailed versions of the descriptions and assessments set out in items (1) to (3) will be needed for preventive measures. In addition to those descriptions and assessments, the following matters should also be covered:
	(10) The conditions and quantities in which hazardous materials are handled;
	(11) A list of the scenarios for the types of industrial accidents with serious effects, to include examples covering the full range of incident size and the possibility of effects from adjacent activities;
	(12) For each scenario, a description of the events which could initiate an industrial accident and the steps whereby it could escalate;
	(13) An assessment, at least in general terms, of the likelihood of each step occurring, taking into account the arrangements in (14);
	(14) A description of the preventive measures in terms of both equipment and procedures designed to minimize the likelihood of each step occurring;
	(15) An assessment of the effects that deviations from normal operating conditions could have, and the consequent arrangements for safe shut-down of the hazardous activity or any part thereof in an emergency, and of the need for staff training to ensure that potentially serious deviations are recognized at an early stage and appropriate action taken;
	(16) An assessment of the extent to which modifications, repair work and maintenance work on the hazardous activity could place the control measures at risk, and the consequent arrangements to ensure that control is maintained.

ANNEX VI

Decision-making on siting pursuant to Article 7

The following illustrates the matters which should be considered pursuant to Article 7:

1. The results of risk analysis and evaluation, including an evaluation pursuant to Annex V of the physical characteristics of the area in which the hazardous activity is being planned;

2. The results of consultations and public participation processes;

3. An analysis of the increase or decrease of the risk caused by any development in the territory of the affected Party in relation to an existing hazardous activity in the territory of the Party of origin;

4. The evaluation of the environmental risks, including any transboundary effects;

5. An evaluation of the new hazardous activities which could be a source of risk;

6. A consideration of the siting of new, and significant modifications to existing hazardous activities at a safe distance from existing centres of population, as well as the establishment of a safety area around hazardous activities; within such areas, developments which would increase the populations at risk, or otherwise increase the severity of the risk, should be closely examined.

ANNEX VII

Emergency preparedness measures pursuant to Article 8

1. All contingency plans, both on- and off-site, should be coordinated to provide a comprehensive and effective response to industrial accidents.

2. The contingency plans should include the actions necessary to localize emergencies and to prevent or minimize their transboundary effects. They should also include arrangements for warning people and, where appropriate, arrangements for their evacuation, other protective or rescue actions and health services.

3. Contingency plans should give on-site personnel, people who might be affected off site and rescue forces, details of technical and organizational procedures which are appropriate for response in the event of an industrial accident capable of having transboundary effects and to prevent and minimize effects on people and the environment, both on and off site.

4. Examples of matters which could be covered by on-site contingency plans include:

(a) Organizational roles and responsibilities on site for dealing with an emergency;

(b) A description of the action which should be taken in the event of an industrial accident, or an imminent threat thereof, in order to control the condition or event, or details of where such a description can be found;

(c) A description of the equipment and resources available;

(d) Arrangements for providing early warning of industrial accidents to the public authority responsible for the off-site emergency response, including the type of information which should be included in an initial warning and the arrangements for providing more detailed information as it becomes available;

(e) Arrangements for training personnel in the duties they will be expected to perform.

5. Examples of matters which could be covered by off-site contingency plans include:

(a) Organizational roles and responsibilities off-site for dealing with an emergency, including how integration with on-site plans is to be achieved;

(b) Methods and procedures to be followed by emergency and medical personnel;

(c) Methods for rapidly determining the affected area;

(d) Arrangements for ensuring that prompt industrial accident notification is made to affected or potentially affected Parties and that that liaison is maintained subsequently;

(e) Identification of resources necessary to implement the plan and the arrangements for coordination;

(f) Arrangements for providing information to the public including, where appropriate, the arrangements for reinforcing and repeating the information provided to the public pursuant to article 9;

(g) Arrangements for training and exercises.

6. Contingency plans could include the measures for: treatment; collection; clean-up; storage; removal and safe disposal of hazardous substances and contaminated material; and restoration.

ANNEX VIII

Information to the public pursuant to Article 9

1. The name of the company, address of the hazardous activity and identification by position held of the person giving the information;

2. An explanation in simple terms of the hazardous activity, including the risks;

3. The common names or the generic names or the general danger classification of the substances and preparations which are involved in the hazardous activity, with an indication of their principal dangerous characteristics;

4. General information resulting from an environmental impact assessment, if available and relevant;

5. The general information relating to the nature of an industrial accident that could possibly occur in the hazardous activity, including its potential effects on the population and the environment;

6. Adequate information on how the affected population will be warned and kept informed in the event of an industrial accident;

7. Adequate information on the actions the affected population should take and on the behaviour they should adopt in the event of an industrial accident;

8. Adequate information on arrangements made regarding the hazardous activity, including liaison

with the emergency services, to deal with industrial accidents, to reduce the severity of the industrial accidents and to mitigate their effects;

9. General information on the emergency services' off-site contingency plan, drawn up to cope with any off-site effects, including the transboundary effects of an industrial accident;

10. General information on special requirements and conditions to which the hazardous activity is subject according to the relevant national regulations and/or administrative provisions, including licensing or authorization systems;

11. Details of where further relevant information can be obtained.

Annex IX

Industrial accident notification systems pursuant to Article 10

1. The industrial accident notification systems shall enable the speediest possible transmission of data and forecasts according to previously determined codes using compatible data-transmission and data-treatment systems for emergency warning and response, and for measures to minimize and contain the consequences of transboundary effects, taking account of different needs at different levels.

2. The industrial accident notification shall include the following:

(*a*) The type and magnitude of the industrial accident, the hazardous substances involved (if known), and the severity of its possible effects;

(*b*) The time of occurrence and exact location of the accident;

(*c*) Such other available information as necessary for an efficient response to the industrial accident.

3. The industrial accident notification shall be supplemented at appropriate intervals, or whenever required, by further relevant information on the development of the situation concerning transboundary effects.

4. Regular tests and reviews of the effectiveness of the industrial accident notification systems shall be undertaken, including the regular training of the personnel involved. Where appropriate, such tests, reviews and training shall be performed jointly.

Annex X

Mutual assistance pursuant to Article 12

1. The overall direction, control, coordination and supervision of the assistance is the responsibility of the requesting Party. The personnel involved in the assisting operation shall act in accordance with the relevant laws of the requesting Party. The appropriate authorities of the requesting Party shall cooperate with the authority designated by the assisting Party, pursuant to Article 17, as being in charge of the immediate operational supervision of the personnel and the equipment provided by the assisting Party.

2. The requesting Party shall, to the extent of its capabilities, provide local facilities and services for the proper and effective administration of the assistance, and shall ensure the protection of personnel, equipment and materials brought into its territory by, or on behalf of, the assisting Party for such a purpose.

3. Unless otherwise agreed by the Parties concerned, assistance shall be provided at the expense of the requesting Party. The assisting Party may at any time waive wholly or partly the reimbursement of costs.

4. The requesting Party shall use its best efforts to afford to the assisting Party and persons acting on its behalf the privileges, immunities or facilities necessary for the expeditious performance of their assistance functions. The requesting Party shall not be required to apply this provision to its own nationals or permanent residents or to afford them the privileges and immunities referred to above.

5. A Party shall, at the request of the requesting or assisting Party, endeavour to facilitate the transit through its territory of duly notified personnel, equipment and

property involved in the assistance to and from the requesting Party.

6. The requesting Party shall facilitate the entry into, stay in and departure from its national territory of duly notified personnel and of equipment and property involved in the assistance.

7. With regard to acts resulting directly from the assistance provided, the requesting Party shall, in respect of the death of or injury to persons, damage to or loss of property, or damage to the environment caused within its territory in the course of the provision of the assistance requested, hold harmless and indemnify the assisting Party or persons acting on its behalf and compensate them for death or injury suffered by them and for loss of or damage to equipment or other property involved in the assistance. The requesting Party shall be responsible for dealing with claims brought by third parties against the assisting Party or persons acting on its behalf.

8. The Parties concerned shall cooperate closely in order to facilitate the settlement of legal proceedings and claims which could result from assistance operations.

9. Any Party may request assistance relating to the medical treatment or the temporary relocation in the territory of another Party of persons involved in an accident.

10. The affected or requesting Party may at any time, after appropriate consultations and by notification, request the termination of assistance received or provided under this Convention. Once such a request has been made, the Parties concerned shall consult one another with a view to making arrangements for the proper termination of the assistance.

ANNEX XI

Exchange of information pursuant to Article 15

Information shall include the following elements, which can also be the subject of multilateral and bilateral cooperation:

(a) Legislative and administrative measures, policies, objectives and priorities for prevention, preparedness and response, scientific activities and technical measures to reduce the risk of industrial accidents from hazardous activities, including the mitigation of transboundary effects;

(b) Measures and contingency plans at the appropriate level affecting other Parties;

(c) Programmes for monitoring, planning, research and development, including their implementation and surveillance;

(d) Measures taken regarding prevention of, preparedness for and response to industrial accidents;

(e) Experience with industrial accidents and cooperation in response to industrial accidents with transboundary effects;

(f) The development and application of the best available technologies for improved environmental protection and safety;

(g) Emergency preparedness and response;

(h) Methods used for the prediction of risks, including criteria for the monitoring and assessment of transboundary effects.

ANNEX XII

Tasks for mutual assistance pursuant to Article 18, paragraph 4

1. *Information and data collection and dissemination*

(a) Establishment and operation of an industrial accident notification system that can provide information on industrial accidents and on experts, in order to involve the experts as rapidly as possible in providing assistance;

(b) Establishment and operation of a data bank for the reception, processing and distribution of necessary information on industrial accidents, including their effects, and also on measures applied and their effectiveness;

(*c*) Elaboration and maintenance of a list of hazardous substances, including their relevant characteristics, and of information on how to deal with those in the event of an industrial accident;

(*d*) Establishment and maintenance of a register of experts to provide consultative and other kinds of assistance regarding preventive, preparedness and response measures, including restoration measures;

(*e*) Maintenance of a list of hazardous activities;

(*f*) Production and maintenance of a list of hazardous substances covered by the provisions of Annex I, Part I.

2.   *Research, training and methodologies*

(*a*) Development and provision of models based on experience from industrial accidents, and scenarios for preventive, preparedness and response measures;

(*b*) Promotion of education and training, organization of international symposia and promotion of cooperation in research and development.

3.   *Technical assistance*

(*a*) Fulfilment of advisory functions aimed at strengthening the ability to apply preventive, preparedness and response measures;

(*b*) Undertaking, at the request of a Party, of inspections of its hazardous activities and the provision of assistance in organizing its national inspections according to the requirements of this Convention.

4.   *Assistance in the case of an emergency*

Provision, at the request of a Party, of assistance by, *inter alia*, sending experts to the site of an industrial accident to provide consultative and other kinds of assistance in response to the industrial accident.

ANNEX XIII

Arbitration

1.   The claimant Party or Parties shall notify the secretariat that the Parties have agreed to submit the dispute to arbitration pursuant to Article 21, paragraph 2 of this Convention. The notification shall state the subject-matter of arbitration and include, in particular, the Articles of this Convention, the interpretation or application of which is at issue. The secretariat shall forward the information received to all Parties to this Convention.

2.   The arbitral tribunal shall consist of three members. Both the claimant Party or Parties and the other Party or Parties to the dispute shall appoint an arbitrator, and the two arbitrators so appointed shall designate by common agreement the third arbitrator, who shall be the president of the arbitral tribunal. The latter shall not be a national of one of the parties to the dispute, nor have his or her usual place of residence in the territory of one of these parties, nor be employed by any of them, nor have dealt with the case in any other capacity.

3.   If the president of the arbitral tribunal has not been designated within two months of the appointment of the second arbitrator, the Executive Secretary of the Economic Commission for Europe shall, at the request of either party to the dispute, designate the president within a further two-month period.

4.   If one of the parties to the dispute does not appoint an arbitrator within two months of the receipt of the request, the other party may so inform the Executive Secretary of the Economic Commission for Europe, who shall designate the president of the arbitral tribunal within a further two-month period. Upon designation,

the president of the arbitral tribunal shall request the party which has not appointed an arbitrator to do so within two months. If it fails to do so within that period, the president shall inform the Executive Secretary of the Economic Commission for Europe, who shall make this appointment within a further two-month period.

5.   The arbitral tribunal shall render its decision in accordance with international law and in accordance with the provisions of this Convention.

6.   Any arbitral tribunal constituted under the provisions set out herein shall draw up its own rules of procedure.

7.   The decisions of the arbitral tribunal, both on procedure and on substance, shall be taken by majority vote of its members.

8.   The tribunal may take all appropriate measures to establish the facts.

9.   The parties to the dispute shall facilitate the work of the arbitral tribunal and, in particular shall, using all means at their disposal:

(*a*) Provide the tribunal with all relevant documents, facilities and information;

(*b*) Enable the tribunal, where necessary, to call witnesses or experts and receive their evidence.

10.   The parties to the dispute and the arbitrators shall protect the confidentiality of any information they

receive in confidence during the proceedings of the arbitral tribunal.

11. The arbitral tribunal may, at the request of one of the parties, recommend interim measures of protection.

12. If one of the parties to the dispute does not appear before the arbitral tribunal or fails to defend its case, the other party may request the tribunal to continue the proceedings and to render its final decision. Absence of a party or failure of a party to defend its case shall not constitute a bar to the proceedings.

13. The arbitral tribunal may hear and determine counter-claims arising directly out of the subject-matter of the dispute.

14. Unless the arbitral tribunal determines otherwise because of the particular circumstances of the case, the expenses of the tribunal, including the remuneration of its members, shall be borne equally by the parties to the dispute. The tribunal shall keep a record of all its expenses and shall furnish a final statement thereof to the parties to the dispute.

15. Any Party to this Convention which has an interest of a legal nature in the subject-matter of the dispute and which may be affected by a decision in the case, may intervene in the proceedings with the consent of the tribunal.

16. The arbitral tribunal shall render its award within five months of the date on which it is established unless it finds it necessary to extend the time-limit for a period which should not exceed five months.

17. The award of the arbitral tribunal shall be accompanied by a statement of reasons. It shall be final and binding upon all parties to the dispute. The award will be transmitted by the arbitral tribunal to the parties to the dispute and to the secretariat. The secretariat will forward the information received to all Parties to this Convention.

18. Any dispute which may arise between the parties concerning the interpretation or execution of the award may be submitted by either party to the arbitral tribunal which made the award or, if the latter cannot be seized thereof, to another tribunal constituted for this purpose in the same manner as the first.

CONVENTION ON THE PROTECTION AND USE OF TRANSBOUNDARY WATERCOURSES AND INTERNATIONAL LAKES

CONVENTION ON THE PROTECTION AND USE OF TRANSBOUNDARY WATERCOURSES AND INTERNATIONAL LAKES

PREAMBLE

The Parties to this Convention,

Mindful that the protection and use of transboundary watercourses and international lakes are important and urgent tasks, the effective accomplishment of which can only be ensured by enhanced cooperation,

Concerned over the existence and threats of adverse effects, in the short or long term, of changes in the conditions of transboundary watercourses and international lakes on the environment, economies and well-being of the member countries of the Economic Commission for Europe (ECE),

Emphasizing the need for strengthened national and international measures to prevent, control and reduce the release of hazardous substances into the aquatic environment and to abate eutrophication and acidification, as well as pollution of the marine environment, in particular coastal areas, from land-based sources,

Commending the efforts already undertaken by the ECE Governments to strengthen cooperation, on bilateral and multilateral levels, for the prevention, control and reduction of transboundary pollution, sustainable water management, conservation of water resources and environmental protection,

Recalling the pertinent provisions and principles of the Declaration of the Stockholm Conference on the Human Environment, the Final Act of the Conference on Security and Cooperation in Europe (CSCE), the Concluding Documents of the Madrid and Vienna Meetings of Representatives of the Participating States of the CSCE, and the Regional Strategy for Environmental Protection and Rational Use of Natural Resources in ECE Member Countries covering the Period up to the Year 2000 and Beyond,

Conscious of the role of the United Nations Economic Commission for Europe in promoting international cooperation for the prevention, control and reduction of transboundary water pollution and sustainable use of transboundary waters, and in this regard recalling the ECE Declaration of Policy on Prevention and Control of Water Pollution, including Transboundary Pollution; the ECE Declaration of Policy on the Rational Use of Water; the ECE Principles Regarding Cooperation in the Field of Transboundary Waters; the ECE Charter on Groundwater Management; and the Code of Conduct on Accidental Pollution of Transboundary Inland Waters,

Referring to decisions I (42) and I (44) adopted by the Economic Commission for Europe at its forty-second and forty-fourth sessions, respectively, and the outcome of the CSCE Meeting on the Protection of the Environment (Sofia, Bulgaria, 16 October -3 November 1989),

Emphasizing that cooperation between member countries in regard to the protection and use of transboundary waters shall be implemented primarily through the elaboration of agreements between countries bordering the same waters, especially where no such agreements have yet been reached,

Have agreed as follows:

Article 1

DEFINITIONS

For the purposes of this Convention,

1. "Transboundary waters" means any surface or ground waters which mark, cross or are located on boundaries between two or more States; wherever transboundary waters flow directly into the sea, these transboundary waters end at a straight line across their respective mouths between points on the low-water line of their banks;

2. "Transboundary impact" means any significant adverse effect on the environment resulting from a change in the conditions of transboundary waters caused by a human activity, the physical origin of which is situated wholly or in part within an area under the jurisdiction of a Party, within an area under the jurisdiction of another Party. Such effects on the environment include effects on human health and safety, flora, fauna, soil, air, water, climate, landscape and historical monuments or other physical structures or the interaction among these factors; they also include effects on the cultural heritage or socio-economic conditions resulting from alterations to those factors;

3. "Party" means, unless the text otherwise indicates, a Contracting Party to this Convention;

4. "Riparian Parties" means the Parties bordering the same transboundary waters;

5. "Joint body" means any bilateral or multilateral commission or other appropriate institutional arrangements for cooperation between the Riparian Parties;

6. "Hazardous substances" means substances which are toxic, carcinogenic, mutagenic, teratogenic or bio-accumulative, especially when they are persistent;

7. "Best available technology" (the definition is contained in annex I to this Convention).

PART I

PROVISIONS RELATING TO ALL PARTIES

Article 2

GENERAL PROVISIONS

1. The Parties shall take all appropriate measures to prevent, control and reduce any transboundary impact.

2. The Parties shall, in particular, take all appropriate measures:

(a) To prevent, control and reduce pollution of waters causing or likely to cause transboundary impact;

(b) To ensure that transboundary waters are used with the aim of ecologically sound and rational water management, conservation of water resources and environmental protection;

(c) To ensure that transboundary waters are used in a reasonable and equitable way, taking into particular account their transboundary character, in the case of activities which cause or are likely to cause transboundary impact;

(d) To ensure conservation and, where necessary, restoration of ecosystems.

3. Measures for the prevention, control and reduction of water pollution shall be taken, where possible, at source.

4. These measures shall not directly or indirectly result in a transfer of pollution to other parts of the environment.

5. In taking the measures referred to in paragraphs 1 and 2 of this article, the Parties shall be guided by the following principles:

(a) The precautionary principle, by virtue of which action to avoid the potential transboundary impact of the release of hazardous substances shall not be postponed on the ground that scientific research has not fully proved a causal link between those substances, on the one hand, and the potential transboundary impact, on the other hand;

(b) The polluter-pays principle, by virtue of which costs of pollution prevention, control and reduction measures shall be borne by the polluter;

(c) Water resources shall be managed so that the needs of the present generation are met without compromising the ability of future generations to meet their own needs.

6. The Riparian Parties shall cooperate on the basis of equality and reciprocity, in particular through bilateral and multilateral agreements, in order to develop harmonized policies, programmes and strategies covering the relevant catchment areas, or parts thereof, aimed at the prevention, control and reduction of transboundary impact and aimed at the protection of the environment of transboundary waters or the environment influenced by such waters, including the marine environment.

7. The application of this Convention shall not lead to the deterioration of environmental conditions nor lead to increased transboundary impact.

8. The provisions of this Convention shall not affect the right of Parties individually or jointly to adopt and implement more stringent measures than those set down in this Convention.

Article 3

PREVENTION, CONTROL AND REDUCTION

1. To prevent, control and reduce transboundary impact, the Parties shall develop, adopt, implement and, as far as possible, render compatible relevant legal, administrative, economic, financial and technical measures, in order to ensure, *inter alia*, that:

(a) The emission of pollutants is prevented, controlled and reduced at source through the application of, *inter alia*, low- and non-waste technology;

(b) Transboundary waters are protected against pollution from point sources through the prior licensing of waste-water discharges by the competent national authorities, and that the authorized discharges are monitored and controlled;

(c) Limits for waste-water discharges stated in permits are based on the best available technology for discharges of hazardous substances;

(d) Stricter requirements, even leading to prohibition in individual cases, are imposed when the quality of the receiving water or the ecosystem so requires;

(e) At least biological treatment or equivalent processes are applied to municipal waste water, where necessary in a step-by-step approach;

(f) Appropriate measures are taken, such as the application of the best available technology, in order to reduce nutrient inputs from industrial and municipal sources;

(g) Appropriate measures and best environmental practices are developed and implemented for the reduction of inputs of nutrients and hazardous substances from diffuse sources, especially where the main sources are from agriculture (guidelines for developing best environmental practices are given in annex II to this Convention);

(h) Environmental impact assessment and other means of assessment are applied;

(i) Sustainable water-resources management, including the application of the ecosystems approach, is promoted;

(j) Contingency planning is developed;

(k) Additional specific measures are taken to prevent the pollution of groundwaters;

(l) The risk of accidental pollution is minimized.

2. To this end, each Party shall set emission limits for discharges from point sources into surface waters based on the best available technology, which are spe-

cifically applicable to individual industrial sectors or industries from which hazardous substances derive. The appropriate measures mentioned in paragraph 1 of this article to prevent, control and reduce the input of hazardous substances from point and diffuse sources into waters, may, *inter alia*, include total or partial prohibition of the production or use of such substances. Existing lists of such industrial sectors or industries and of such hazardous substances in international conventions or regulations, which are applicable in the area covered by this Convention, shall be taken into account.

3.   In addition, each Party shall define, where appropriate, water-quality objectives and adopt water-quality criteria for the purpose of preventing, controlling and reducing transboundary impact. General guidance for developing such objectives and criteria is given in annex III to this Convention. When necessary, the Parties shall endeavour to update this annex.

Article 4

MONITORING

The Parties shall establish programmes for monitoring the conditions of transboundary waters.

Article 5

RESEARCH AND DEVELOPMENT

The Parties shall cooperate in the conduct of research into and development of effective techniques for the prevention, control and reduction of transboundary impact. To this effect, the Parties shall, on a bilateral and/or multilateral basis, taking into account research activities pursued in relevant international forums, endeavour to initiate or intensify specific research programmes, where necessary, aimed, *inter alia*, at:

(*a*) Methods for the assessment of the toxicity of hazardous substances and the noxiousness of pollutants;

(*b*) Improved knowledge on the occurrence, distribution and environmental effects of pollutants and the processes involved;

(*c*) The development and application of environmentally sound technologies, production and consumption patterns;

(*d*) The phasing out and/or substitution of substances likely to have transboundary impact;

(*e*) Environmentally sound methods of disposal of hazardous substances;

(*f*) Special methods for improving the conditions of transboundary waters;

(*g*) The development of environmentally sound water-construction works and water-regulation techniques;

(*h*) The physical and financial assessment of damage resulting from transboundary impact.

The results of these research programmes shall be exchanged among the Parties in accordance with article 6 of this Convention.

Article 6

EXCHANGE OF INFORMATION

The Parties shall provide for the widest exchange of information, as early as possible, on issues covered by the provisions of this Convention.

Article 7

RESPONSIBILITY AND LIABILITY

The Parties shall support appropriate international efforts to elaborate rules, criteria and procedures in the field of responsibility and liability.

Article 8

PROTECTION OF INFORMATION

The provisions of this Convention shall not affect the rights or the obligations of Parties in accordance with their national legal systems and applicable supranational regulations to protect information related to industrial and commercial secrecy, including intellectual property, or national security.

PART II

PROVISIONS RELATING TO RIPARIAN PARTIES

Article 9

BILATERAL AND MULTILATERAL COOPERATION

1.   The Riparian Parties shall on the basis of equality and reciprocity enter into bilateral or multilateral agreements or other arrangements, where these do not yet exist, or adapt existing ones, where necessary to eliminate the contradictions with the basic principles of this Convention, in order to define their mutual relations and conduct regarding the prevention, control and reduction of transboundary impact. The Riparian Parties shall specify the catchment area, or part(s) thereof, subject to cooperation. These agreements or arrangements shall embrace relevant issues covered by this Convention, as well as any other issues on which the Riparian Parties may deem it necessary to cooperate.

2.   The agreements or arrangements mentioned in paragraph 1 of this article shall provide for the establishment of joint bodies. The tasks of these joint bodies shall be, *inter alia*, and without prejudice to relevant existing agreements or arrangements, the following:

(a) To collect, compile and evaluate data in order to identify pollution sources likely to cause transboundary impact;

(b) To elaborate joint monitoring programmes concerning water quality and quantity;

(c) To draw up inventories and exchange information on the pollution sources mentioned in paragraph 2 (a) of this article;

(d) To elaborate emission limits for waste water and evaluate the effectiveness of control programmes;

(e) To elaborate joint water-quality objectives and criteria having regard to the provisions of article 3, paragraph 3 of this Convention, and to propose relevant measures for maintaining and, where necessary, improving the existing water quality;

(f) To develop concerted action programmes for the reduction of pollution loads from both point sources (e.g. municipal and industrial sources) and diffuse sources (particularly from agriculture);

(g) To establish warning and alarm procedures;

(h) To serve as a forum for the exchange of information on existing and planned uses of water and related installations that are likely to cause transboundary impact;

(i) To promote cooperation and exchange of information on the best available technology in accordance with the provisions of article 13 of this Convention, as well as to encourage cooperation in scientific research programmes;

(j) To participate in the implementation of environmental impact assessments relating to transboundary waters, in accordance with appropriate international regulations.

3. In cases where a coastal State, being Party to this Convention, is directly and significantly affected by transboundary impact, the Riparian Parties can, if they all so agree, invite that coastal State to be involved in an appropriate manner in the activities of multilateral joint bodies established by Parties riparian to such transboundary waters.

4. Joint bodies according to this Convention shall invite joint bodies, established by coastal States for the protection of the marine environment directly affected by transboundary impact, to cooperate in order to harmonize their work and to prevent, control and reduce the transboundary impact.

5. Where two or more joint bodies exist in the same catchment area, they shall endeavour to coordinate their activities in order to strengthen the prevention, control and reduction of transboundary impact within that catchment area.

Article 10

CONSULTATIONS

Consultations shall be held between the Riparian Parties on the basis of reciprocity, good faith and good-neighbourliness, at the request of any such Party. Such consultations shall aim at cooperation regarding the is-

sues covered by the provisions of this Convention. Any such consultations shall be conducted through a joint body established under article 9 of this Convention, where one exists.

Article 11

JOINT MONITORING AND ASSESSMENT

1. In the framework of general cooperation mentioned in article 9 of this Convention, or specific arrangements, the Riparian Parties shall establish and implement joint programmes for monitoring the conditions of transboundary waters, including floods and ice drifts, as well as transboundary impact.

2. The Riparian Parties shall agree upon pollution parameters and pollutants whose discharges and concentration in transboundary waters shall be regularly monitored.

3. The Riparian Parties shall, at regular intervals, carry out joint or coordinated assessments of the conditions of transboundary waters and the effectiveness of measures taken for the prevention, control and reduction of transboundary impact. The results of these assessments shall be made available to the public in accordance with the provisions set out in article 16 of this Convention.

4. For these purposes, the Riparian Parties shall harmonize rules for the setting up and operation of monitoring programmes, measurement systems, devices, analytical techniques, data processing and evaluation procedures, and methods for the registration of pollutants discharged.

Article 12

COMMON RESEARCH AND DEVELOPMENT

In the framework of general cooperation mentioned in article 9 of this Convention, or specific arrangements, the Riparian Parties shall undertake specific research and development activities in support of achieving and maintaining the water-quality objectives and criteria which they have agreed to set and adopt.

Article 13

EXCHANGE OF INFORMATION BETWEEN RIPARIAN PARTIES

1. The Riparian Parties shall, within the framework of relevant agreements or other arrangements according to article 9 of this Convention, exchange reasonably available data, inter alia, on:

(a) Environmental conditions of transboundary waters;

(b) Experience gained in the application and operation of best available technology and results of research and development;

(*c*) Emission and monitoring data;

(*d*) Measures taken and planned to be taken to prevent, control and reduce transboundary impact;

(*e*) Permits or regulations for waste-water discharges issued by the competent authority or appropriate body.

2. In order to harmonize emission limits, the Riparian Parties shall undertake the exchange of information on their national regulations.

3. If a Riparian Party is requested by another Riparian Party to provide data or information that is not available, the former shall endeavour to comply with the request but may condition its compliance upon the payment, by the requesting Party, of reasonable charges for collecting and, where appropriate, processing such data or information.

4. For the purposes of the implementation of this Convention, the Riparian Parties shall facilitate the exchange of best available technology, particularly through the promotion of: the commercial exchange of available technology; direct industrial contacts and cooperation, including joint ventures; the exchange of information and experience; and the provision of technical assistance. The Riparian Parties shall also undertake joint training programmes and the organization of relevant seminars and meetings.

Article 14

WARNING AND ALARM SYSTEMS

The Riparian Parties shall without delay inform each other about any critical situation that may have transboundary impact. The Riparian Parties shall set up, where appropriate, and operate coordinated or joint communication, warning and alarm systems with the aim of obtaining and transmitting information. These systems shall operate on the basis of compatible data transmission and treatment procedures and facilities to be agreed upon by the Riparian Parties. The Riparian Parties shall inform each other about competent authorities or points of contact designated for this purpose.

Article 15

MUTUAL ASSISTANCE

1. If a critical situation should arise, the Riparian Parties shall provide mutual assistance upon request, following procedures to be established in accordance with paragraph 2 of this article.

2. The Riparian Parties shall elaborate and agree upon procedures for mutual assistance addressing, *inter alia*, the following issues:

(*a*) The direction, control, coordination and supervision of assistance;

(*b*) Local facilities and services to be rendered by the Party requesting assistance, including, where necessary, the facilitation of border-crossing formalities;

(*c*) Arrangements for holding harmless, indemnifying and/or compensating the assisting Party and/or its personnel, as well as for transit through territories of third Parties, where necessary;

(*d*) Methods of reimbursing assistance services.

Article 16

PUBLIC INFORMATION

1. The Riparian Parties shall ensure that information on the conditions of transboundary waters, measures taken or planned to be taken to prevent, control and reduce transboundary impact, and the effectiveness of those measures, is made available to the public. For this purpose, the Riparian Parties shall ensure that the following information is made available to the public:

(*a*) Water-quality objectives;

(*b*) Permits issued and the conditions required to be met;

(*c*) Results of water and effluent sampling carried out for the purposes of monitoring and assessment, as well as results of checking compliance with the water-quality objectives or the permit conditions.

2. The Riparian Parties shall ensure that this information shall be available to the public at all reasonable times for inspection free of charge, and shall provide members of the public with reasonable facilities for obtaining from the Riparian Parties, on payment of reasonable charges, copies of such information.

PART III

INSTITUTIONAL AND FINAL PROVISIONS

Article 17

MEETING OF PARTIES

1. The first meeting of the Parties shall be convened no later than one year after the date of the entry into force of this Convention. Thereafter, ordinary meetings shall be held every three years, or at shorter intervals as laid down in the rules of procedure. The Parties shall hold an extraordinary meeting if they so decide in the course of an ordinary meeting or at the written request of any Party, provided that, within six months of it being communicated to all Parties, the said request is supported by at least one third of the Parties.

2. At their meetings, the Parties shall keep under continuous review the implementation of this Convention, and, with this purpose in mind, shall:

(*a*) Review the policies for and methodological approaches to the protection and use of transboundary waters of the Parties with a view to further improving the protection and use of transboundary waters;

(*b*) Exchange information regarding experience gained in concluding and implementing bilateral and multilateral agreements or other arrangements regarding the protection and use of transboundary waters to which one or more of the Parties are party;

(c) Seek, where appropriate, the services of relevant ECE bodies as well as other competent international bodies and specific committees in all aspects pertinent to the achievement of the purposes of this Convention;

(d) At their first meeting, consider and by consensus adopt rules of procedure for their meetings;

(e) Consider and adopt proposals for amendments to this Convention;

(f) Consider and undertake any additional action that may be required for the achievement of the purposes of this Convention.

Article 18

RIGHT TO VOTE

1. Except as provided for in paragraph 2 of this article, each Party to this Convention shall have one vote.

2. Regional economic integration organizations, in matters within their competence, shall exercise their right to vote with a number of votes equal to the number of their member States which are Parties to this Convention. Such organizations shall not exercise their right to vote if their member States exercise theirs, and vice versa.

Article 19

SECRETARIAT

The Executive Secretary of the Economic Commission for Europe shall carry out the following secretariat functions:

(a) The convening and preparing of meetings of the Parties;

(b) The transmission to the Parties of reports and other information received in accordance with the provisions of this Convention;

(c) The performance of such other functions as may be determined by the Parties.

Article 20

ANNEXES

Annexes to this Convention shall constitute an integral part thereof.

Article 21

AMENDMENTS TO THE CONVENTION

1. Any Party may propose amendments to this Convention.

2. Proposals for amendments to this Convention shall be considered at a meeting of the Parties.

3. The text of any proposed amendment to this Convention shall be submitted in writing to the Executive Secretary of the Economic Commission for Europe, who shall communicate it to all Parties at least ninety days before the meeting at which it is proposed for adoption.

4. An amendment to the present Convention shall be adopted by consensus of the representatives of the Parties to this Convention present at a meeting of the Parties, and shall enter into force for the Parties to the Convention which have accepted it on the ninetieth day after the date on which two thirds of those Parties have deposited with the Depositary their instruments of acceptance of the amendment. The amendment shall enter into force for any other Party on the ninetieth day after the date on which that Party deposits its instrument of acceptance of the amendment.

Article 22

SETTLEMENT OF DISPUTES

1. If a dispute arises between two or more Parties about the interpretation or application of this Convention, they shall seek a solution by negotiation or by any other means of dispute settlement acceptable to the parties to the dispute.

2. When signing, ratifying, accepting, approving or acceding to this Convention, or at any time thereafter, a Party may declare in writing to the Depositary that, for a dispute not resolved in accordance with paragraph 1 of this article, it accepts one or both of the following means of dispute settlement as compulsory in relation to any Party accepting the same obligation:

(a) Submission of the dispute to the International Court of Justice;

(b) Arbitration in accordance with the procedure set out in annex IV.

3. If the parties to the dispute have accepted both means of dispute settlement referred to in paragraph 2 of this article, the dispute may be submitted only to the International Court of Justice, unless the parties agree otherwise.

Article 23

SIGNATURE

This Convention shall be open for signature at Helsinki from 17 to 18 March 1992 inclusive, and thereafter at United Nations Headquarters in New York until 18 September 1992, by States members of the Economic Commission for Europe as well as States having consultative status with the Economic Commission for Europe pursuant to paragraph 8 of Economic and Social Council resolution 36 (IV) of 28 March 1947, and by regional economic integration organizations constituted by sovereign States members of the Economic Commission for Europe to which their member States have transferred competence over matters governed by this Convention, including the competence to enter into treaties in respect of these matters.

Article 24

DEPOSITARY

The Secretary-General of the United Nations shall act as the Depositary of this Convention.

Article 25

RATIFICATION, ACCEPTANCE, APPROVAL AND ACCESSION

1. This Convention shall be subject to ratification, acceptance or approval by signatory States and regional economic integration organizations.

2. This Convention shall be open for accession by the States and organizations referred to in article 23.

3. Any organization referred to in article 23 which becomes a Party to this Convention without any of its member States being a Party shall be bound by all the obligations under this Convention. In the case of such organizations, one or more of whose member States is a Party to this Convention, the organization and its member States shall decide on their respective responsibilities for the performance of their obligations under this Convention. In such cases, the organization and the member States shall not be entitled to exercise rights under this Convention concurrently.

4. In their instruments of ratification, acceptance, approval or accession, the regional economic integration organizations referred to in article 23 shall declare the extent of their competence with respect to the matters governed by this Convention. These organizations shall also inform the Depositary of any substantial modification to the extent of their competence.

Article 26

ENTRY INTO FORCE

1. This Convention shall enter into force on the ninetieth day after the date of deposit of the sixteenth instrument of ratification, acceptance, approval or accession.

2. For the purposes of paragraph 1 of this article, any instrument deposited by a regional economic integration organization shall not be counted as additional to those deposited by States members of such an organization.

3. For each State or organization referred to in article 23 which ratifies, accepts or approves this Convention or accedes thereto after the deposit of the sixteenth instrument of ratification, acceptance, approval or accession, the Convention shall enter into force on the ninetieth day after the date of deposit by such State or organization of its instrument of ratification, acceptance, approval or accession.

Article 27

WITHDRAWAL

At any time after three years from the date on which this Convention has come into force with respect to a Party, that Party may withdraw from the Convention by giving written notification to the Depositary. Any such withdrawal shall take effect on the ninetieth day after the date of its receipt by the Depositary.

Article 28

AUTHENTIC TEXTS

The original of this Convention, of which the English, French and Russian texts are equally authentic, shall be deposited with the Secretary-General of the United Nations.

IN WITNESS WHEREOF the undersigned, being duly authorized thereto, have signed this Convention.

DONE at Helsinki, this seventeenth day of March one thousand nine hundred and ninety-two.

ANNEXES

ANNEX I

Definition of the term "best available technology"

1. The term "best available technology" is taken to mean the latest stage of development of processes, facilities or methods of operation which indicate the practical suitability of a particular measure for limiting discharges, emissions and waste. In determining whether a set of processes, facilities and methods of operation constitute the best available technology in general or individual cases, special consideration is given to:

(*a*) Comparable processes, facilities or methods of operation which have recently been successfully tried out;

(*b*) Technological advances and changes in scientific knowledge and understanding;

(*c*) The economic feasibility of such technology;

(*d*) Time limits for installation in both new and existing plants;

(*e*) The nature and volume of the discharges and effluents concerned;

(*f*) Low- and non-waste technology.

2. It therefore follows that what is "best available technology" for a particular process will change with time in the light of technological advances, economic and social factors, as well as in the light of changes in scientific knowledge and understanding.

ANNEX II

Guidelines for developing best environmental practices

1. In selecting for individual cases the most appropriate combination of measures which may constitute the best environmental practice, the following graduated range of measures should be considered:

(*a*) Provision of information and education to the public and to users about the environmental consequences of the choice of particular activities and products, their use and ultimate disposal;

(*b*) The development and application of codes of good environmental practice which cover all aspects of the product's life;

(*c*) Labels informing users of environmental risks related to a product, its use and ultimate disposal;

(*d*) Collection and disposal systems available to the public;

(*e*) Recycling, recovery and reuse;

(*f*) Application of economic instruments to activities, products or groups of products;

(*g*) A system of licensing, which involves a range of restrictions or a ban.

2. In determining what combination of measures constitute best environmental practices, in general or in individual cases, particular consideration should be given to:

(*a*) The environmental hazard of:

  (i) The product;

  (ii) The product's production;

  (iii) The product's use;

  (iv) The product's ultimate disposal;

(*b*) Substitution by less polluting processes or substances;

(*c*) Scale of use;

(*d*) Potential environmental benefit or penalty of substitute materials or activities;

(*e*) Advances and changes in scientific knowledge and understanding;

(*f*) Time limits for implementation;

(*g*) Social and economic implications.

3. It therefore follows that best environmental practices for a particular source will change with time in the light of technological advances, economic and social factors, as well as in the light of changes in scientific knowledge and understanding.

ANNEX III

Guidelines for developing water-quality objectives and criteria

Water-quality objectives and criteria shall:

(*a*) Take into account the aim of maintaining and, where necessary, improving the existing water quality;

(*b*) Aim at the reduction of average pollution loads (in particular hazardous substances) to a certain degree within a certain period of time;

(*c*) Take into account specific water-quality requirements (raw water for drinking-water purposes, irrigation, etc.);

(*d*) Take into account specific requirements regarding sensitive and specially protected waters and their environment, e.g. lakes and groundwater resources;

(*e*) Be based on the application of ecological classification methods and chemical indices for the medium- and long-term review of water-quality maintenance and improvement;

(*f*) Take into account the degree to which objectives are reached and the additional protective measures, based on emission limits, which may be required in individual cases.

ANNEX IV

Arbitration

1. In the event of a dispute being submitted for arbitration pursuant to article 22, paragraph 2 of this Convention, a party or parties shall notify the secretariat of the subject-matter of arbitration and indicate, in particular, the articles of this Convention whose interpretation or application is at issue. The secretariat shall forward the information received to all Parties to this Convention.

2. The arbitral tribunal shall consist of three members. Both the claimant party or parties and the other party or parties to the dispute shall appoint an arbitrator, and the two arbitrators so appointed shall designate by common agreement the third arbitrator, who shall be the president of the arbitral tribunal. The latter shall not be a national of one of the parties to the dispute, nor have his or her usual place of residence in the territory of one of these parties, nor be employed by any of them, nor have dealt with the case in any other capacity.

3. If the president of the arbitral tribunal has not been designated within two months of the appointment of the second arbitrator, the Executive Secretary of the Economic Commission for Europe shall, at the request of either party to the dispute, designate the president within a further two-month period.

4. If one of the parties to the dispute does not appoint an arbitrator within two months of the receipt of the request, the other party may so inform the Executive Secretary of the Economic Commission for Europe, who shall designate the president of the arbitral tribunal within a further two-month period. Upon designation, the president of the arbitral tribunal shall request the party which has not appointed an arbitrator to do so within two months. If it fails to do so within that period, the president shall so inform the Executive Secretary of

the Economic Commission for Europe, who shall make this appointment within a further two-month period.

5. The arbitral tribunal shall render its decision in accordance with international law and the provisions of this Convention.

6. Any arbitral tribunal constituted under the provisions set out in this annex shall draw up its own rules of procedure.

7. The decisions of the arbitral tribunal, both on procedure and on substance, shall be taken by majority vote of its members.

8. The tribunal may take all appropriate measures to establish the facts.

9. The parties to the dispute shall facilitate the work of the arbitral tribunal and, in particular, using all means at their disposal, shall:

(*a*) Provide it with all relevant documents, facilities and information;

(*b*) Enable it, where necessary, to call witnesses or experts and receive their evidence.

10. The parties and the arbitrators shall protect the confidentiality of any information they receive in confidence during the proceedings of the arbitral tribunal.

11. The arbitral tribunal may, at the request of one of the parties, recommend interim measures of protection.

12. If one of the parties to the dispute does not appear before the arbitral tribunal or fails to defend its case, the other party may request the tribunal to continue the proceedings and to render its final decision. Absence

of a party or failure of a party to defend its case shall not constitute a bar to the proceedings.

13. The arbitral tribunal may hear and determine counter-claims arising directly out of the subject-matter of the dispute.

14. Unless the arbitral tribunal determines otherwise because of the particular circumstances of the case, the expenses of the tribunal, including the remuneration of its members, shall be borne by the parties to the dispute in equal shares. The tribunal shall keep a record of all its expenses, and shall furnish a final statement thereof to the parties.

15. Any Party to this Convention which has an interest of a legal nature in the subject-matter of the dispute, and which may be affected by a decision in the case, may intervene in the proceedings with the consent of the tribunal.

16. The arbitral tribunal shall render its award within five months of the date on which it is established, unless it finds it necessary to extend the time limit for a period which should not exceed five months.

17. The award of the arbitral tribunal shall be accompanied by a statement of reasons. It shall be final and binding upon all parties to the dispute. The award will be transmitted by the arbitral tribunal to the parties to the dispute and to the secretariat. The secretariat will forward the information received to all Parties to this Convention.

18. Any dispute which may arise between the parties concerning the interpretation or execution of the award may be submitted by either party to the arbitral tribunal which made the award or, if the latter cannot be seized thereof, to another tribunal constituted for this purpose in the same manner as the first.